*Sound of the Moon* and Other Plays by
Myung-Wha Kim

AF215161

# *Sound of the Moon* and Other Plays by Myung-Wha Kim

Myung-Wha Kim

Translated from Korean into English by Walter Byongsok Chon

English Language Translation Consultant: Anne M. Hamilton

*methuen* | drama

LONDON • NEW YORK • OXFORD • NEW DELHI • SYDNEY

METHUEN DRAMA
Bloomsbury Publishing Plc, 50 Bedford Square, London, WC1B 3DP, UK
Bloomsbury Publishing Inc, 1359 Broadway, New York, NY 10018, USA
Bloomsbury Publishing Ireland, 29 Earlsfort Terrace, Dublin 2, D02 AY28, Ireland

BLOOMSBURY, METHUEN DRAMA and the Methuen Drama logo are trademarks of Bloomsbury
Publishing Plc

First published in Great Britain 2026

Copyright © Byongsok Chon, and Contributors, 2026
*Birds Don't Use a Crosswalk* © Myung-Wha Kim, 1998
*Birds Don't Use a Crosswalk* English translation © Byongsok Chon, 2026
*Oedipus: The Fate of the Story* © Myung-Wha Kim, 2000
*Oedipus: The Fate of the Story* English translation © Byongsok Chon, 2026
*Sound of the Moon* © Myung-Wha Kim, 2006
*Sound of the Moon* English translation © Byongsok Chon, 2026
*The Wind's Desire* © Myung-Wha Kim, 2007
*The Wind's Desire* English translation © Byongsok Chon, 2020–2026

Walter Byongsok Chon has asserted his right under the Copyright, Designs and Patents Act, 1988, to be
identified as author of this work.

The Publisher would like to thank The Daesan Foundation for their support of this collection.

For legal purposes the Acknowledgments on p. vi constitute an extension of this copyright page.

Cover design by Jade Barnett
Cover images: Gabriel Tovar / Unsplash (main image) © Natalia-flurno / Getty Images (background texture)
Author photograph © Hanmin Kang

All rights reserved. No part of this publication may be: i) reproduced or transmitted in any form, electronic or
mechanical, including photocopying, recording or by means of any information storage or retrieval system
without prior permission in writing from the publishers; or ii) used or reproduced in any way for the training,
development or operation of artificial intelligence (AI) technologies, including generative AI technologies. The
rights holders expressly reserve this publication from the text and data mining exception as per Article 4(3) of
the Digital Single Market Directive (EU) 2019/790.

Bloomsbury Publishing Plc does not have any control over, or responsibility for, any third-party websites
referred to or in this book. All internet addresses given in this book were correct at the time of going to press.
The author and publisher regret any inconvenience caused if addresses have changed or sites have ceased to
exist, but can accept no responsibility for any such changes.

A catalogue record for this book is available from the British Library.

A catalog record for this book is available from the Library of Congress.

ISBN:  HB:      978-1-3505-7272-0
       PB:      978-1-3505-7271-3
       ePDF:    978-1-3505-7273-7
       eBook:   978-1-3505-7274-4

Series: Methuen Drama Play Collections

Typeset by RefineCatch Limited, Bungay, Suffolk
Printed and bound in Great Britain

For product safety related questions contact productsafety@bloomsbury.com.

To find out more about our authors and books visit www.bloomsbury.com and sign up for our newsletters.

# Contents

# Acknowledgments

The translator and English language consultant thank the Daesan Foundation for awarding them the 2022 Grant for the Translation of Korean Literary Works, with which they completed *An English Theatrical Translation of Korean Plays by Myung-Wha Kim*.

The translator and English language translation consultant were each awarded a Fellowship by the Bogliasco Foundation, and completed Spring 2024 Residencies in Bogliasco, Italy. *An English Theatrical Translation of Korean Plays by Myung-Wha Kim* was created with the support of a Bogliasco Foundation Fellowship.

# About *Sound of the Moon* and Other Plays by Myung-Wha Kim

This collection contains four plays by contemporary Korean playwright Myung-Wha Kim, translated by Walter Byongsok Chon, in collaboration with English language consultant Anne Hamilton. The plays—*Birds Don't Use a Crosswalk*, *Oedipus: The Fate of the Story*, *Sound of the Moon*, and *The Wind's Desire*—were chosen in a consultation between the author and the translator. This collection includes several genres exploring Korean history, culture, and sentiments, and represents the author's masterful artistic expressions and achievements.

With the global popularity and recognition of Korean culture, it is imperative that Korean theatre should be introduced to international audiences and readers as well. With the recent success of Korean culture—K-pop (BTS, BLACKPINK), K-film (*Parasite*, *Past Lives*), and K-literature (2024 Nobel Prize winner Han Kang), to name a few—interest in Korean culture as a whole is growing. This collection presents some of the finest contemporary Korean plays, and it is the first translated collection of Korean plays written by a female playwright.

In the context of contemporary Korean theatre, Myung-Wha Kim occupies a distinctive place as an acclaimed playwright, critic, and director as well as the artistic director of her own company The Nanhee. She made her playwriting debut with *Birds Don't Use a Crosswalk*, which won the Samsung Literary Award for Best Play in 1997. Her plays include *First Birthday*, *Cello and Ketchup*, *Café Shinpa*, *Oedipus: The Fate of the Story*, *Yi Kwang-Su's Dream and Flower*, *Sound of the Moon*, *The End of the Royal Palace Dining Hall*, *Dionysus Under the Magnolia*, *Cold Noodles*, and *Mimaji!*. Her plays have been published in their original language in four collected volumes (ZMANZ Press, Korea). She won numerous awards including the Cha Beom-Seok Theater Award, Daesan Literary Award, Dong-A Theater Award, the Grand Prize in the Asahi Shimbun Theatrical Arts Award, and the Yeo Seok-Gi Theater Critic Award. She founded Nanhee Theatre Company in 2018, which became The Nanhee in 2020, and took up directing. With The Nanhee, her direction credits include *Dionysus Under the Magnolia* and *Mimaji!*, two pieces exploring the origin of theatre, and *Hamlet: The Dead Man Tells No Tales*.

During my trip from the U.S. to South Korea in 2019, one of my objectives was to find Korean plays to translate into English. The enthusiastic audience response to my first produced English translation—Sam-Shik Pai's *Inching Towards Yeolha* (배삼식, <열하일기만보>), at Columbia University in 2010—had made me excited about the appeal a Korean play in English translation can have upon audiences who might not be familiar with the play or playwright or with the cultural context and the nuance of the language. Theatrical translation, both from Korean into English and from English into Korean, became for me a way to immerse myself in the cultures which make up my life and to connect with each of them in a deeper and more productive way. It was Professor Mihee Kim at the School of Drama at the Korea National University of Arts who recommended to me the plays of Myung-Wha Kim.

Upon the recommendation, I purchased Myung-Wha Kim's collected plays and was mesmerized by the scope of her topics, forms, and styles. I found particularly intriguing her play *The Wind's Desire* from 2007, and contacted the playwright for permission to translate it. This permission encouraged me to seek opportunities to translate more of her work, as I contemplated which plays to translate and envisioned how the translation could appeal to an English-speaking audience.

In 2022, the Daesan Foundation awarded me and the English translation consultant Anne Hamilton the Grant for the Translation of Korean Literary Works to translate a collection of Myung-Wha Kim's plays. Among her broad body of works, the playwright and I chose four plays that we believed could best represent her works to English-speaking readers and audiences. They represented a variety of subject matters, genres, languages, and forms. *Birds Don't Use a Crosswalk* (1998) explores the role of theatre in society, wherein the protagonist is a director who returns to his college to helm a production. It navigates the tumultuous historical trajectory from the 1980s to present-day Korea. The second play *Oedipus: The Fate of the Story* (2000) is an adaptation of Sophocles' *Oedipus* and explores the political and personal affairs that might have occurred behind closed doors. The third play *Sound of the Moon* (2006), set in the late sixth century during Korea's Three Kingdoms period, portrays the romance between an aspiring *gayageum* musician and the Princess of Silla, which creates intrigues with diplomatic, cultural, and sociopolitical implications. And *The Wind's Desire* (2007) tells the story of a television writer in modern-day Seoul, who financially supports her family abroad and starts an affair with a young photographer. While these plays reflect specific Korean sentiments and sensibilities, the playwright and I believe that these stories have international appeal. The questions they pose about art, love, family, politics, and society transcend cultural and national boundaries.

*Birds Don't Use a Crosswalk* premiered at Theatre Aroong-Guji in Seoul, Korea, under the direction of Tae-seok Oh in 1998. In this play, Ji-Hwan, a Ph.D. student, gets a phone call from his college theatre club. The club just lost its director and are in desperate need of a new one to direct their production of *Waiting for Godot*. Ji-Hwan accepts the offer reluctantly, because of the trauma he experienced in his college days in the 1980s. Once he meets the members of the theatre club, conflict immediately ensues, between Ji-Hwan's authoritarian approach to directing—a subconscious remnant of 1980s militaristic culture, when students regularly protested against the military regime—and the individualistic and democratic culture of the current college students. Haunted by the death of his friend during the protest in his college days, Ji-Hwan continues to explore what theatre can offer society—what value and meaning there is in mounting this production—and how he can manage to work with the next generation of theatre makers.

*Oedipus: The Fate of the Story* premiered at the ARKO Arts Theater as part of the 2000 Seoul Theater Festival, under the direction of Gwangbo Kim. The play's title at the premiere was *Oedipus: The Human*. The play became *Oedipus: The Fate of the Story* for its publication in 2018, after the playwright updated the play and included in it her contemplation on the role, struggle, and power of art in an oppressive society. This play starts with the Old Poet narrating the story of Oedipus the King defeating the Sphinx and becoming the King of Thebes. In the Old Poet's story, Thebes has been suffering from a drought for three years. The Senior Ministers urge Oedipus for more prayer for rain, while Oedipus is focused on the construction of a dam with his young crew. Behind Oedipus' back, Creon, Oedipus' brother-in-law, conspires with the Senior Ministers and the priest Tiresias to take down the king and become regent himself. Tiresias delivers the oracle that finding the murderer of the previous king, King Laius, is the only way to end the drought. Creon and Tiresias frame Oedipus for the murder, have him arrested, and put him on trial. As Oedipus and his followers fight for justice, the truth of Oedipus' origin is slowly revealed to devastating consequences. The play moves back and forth in time as the Old Poet recalls living through those times and passes on the torch of storytelling to the Boy who was enchanted by the story.

*Sound of the Moon* premiered at Mary Hall in Sogang University as part of the 2006 Seoul Theater Festival, under the direction of Jung-Hee Park. This play is set in mid-sixth-century Korea, where the Gaya Confederacy is in peril and the Silla Kingdom emerges as a new empire. This play is a period drama, portraying Wooreuk, the creator of the traditional Korean stringed instrument the *gayageum*, the Princess of Silla, and their musicians and families, in the context of changing sociological and political order. Wooreuk's master student Yimoon has a conflict with his master about the purpose of art. Wooreuk plays for the mastery of sound itself, while Yimoon wants to play for the people. This conflict causes Yimoon to leave Gaya. He finds himself at the royal palace in Silla and, concealing his true identity as a Gayan musician, falls in love with the Princess of Silla. The Princess is deaf and finds comfort in Yimoon's lessons about sound. As their love is about to blossom, Yimoon is accused of treachery, and once his identity is discovered, the princess gives orders to make him deaf and blind and kicks him out of the palace. Deaf, blind, and devastated by the loss of love, Yimoon finds his way back home.

*The Wind's Desire* premiered at the Sanwoollim Theatre in Seoul, Korea, under the direction of Young-Woong Lim in 2007. This play portrays a middle-aged married television writer ("She"), her lover, a photographer who is twenty years her junior ("He"), and her television producer friend ("Her Friend"), all living in modern-day Seoul, Korea. The play follows the affair between "She" and "He," while "She" tries to pen her next soap opera. "She" needs a hit show, a story that can connect with a broad demographic, and she finds her real-life affair making its way into the story she is creating. "Her Friend," unaware of the affair and needing desperately to produce a hit show, questions the plausibility of an affair between a middle-aged woman and a man twenty years younger. "She" is also a "wild goose mom," who sends money to her husband and child who are in Los Angeles for the child's education. "She" tries to balance her affair, her writing, her friendship, and her family. "She" finds her art, her desire, her public life, and her secret life becoming all tangled up, leading her into uncertain directions with unexpected consequences.

My objective in translation for the stage is, broadly speaking, breathing full life into the words to be spoken and embodied on stage. For this purpose, I say the original line out loud to myself multiple times, until it feels natural in my own voice. As I translate, I repeat this process until I find the right expression, tone, and cadence in the translated language. It is also a constant negotiation between how to make the strange familiar – and how much – and where and how to let the strangeness speak for itself and leave it as something unfamiliar.

In translating these plays, there were particular challenges because, in three of these plays, the Korean setting and phenomenon are very specific and essential for the storytelling. In *Birds Don't Use a Crosswalk*, the military regime that Korea went through in the 1980s and the cultural shift in the 1990s serve as the main cause of conflict between Ji-Hwan and the creative team. In *Sound of the Moon*, the *gayageum* provides the central musical motif, as there are several scenes that require the actors to play this instrument. While the shifting national and political landscape tremendously impacts the onstage action and fate of the characters, the actual historical record of this period is not complete and consistent. Wooreuk and the Princess are historical figures, and their actions and personal circumstances are imagined and given substance based on the playwright's research of Korean history. *The Wind's Desire* portrays the wild goose daddy phenomenon—referring to a father who works in Korea while sending his wife and children to an English-speaking country for the children's education. This play reverses the gender roles. The affair between an older woman and a younger man also goes against the more familiar trope of older man with younger woman. The middle-aged woman's desire—both for the return of spring and for artistic achievement—takes center stage. The "Wind" in the title, in Korean, directly refers to her affair. While *Oedipus: The Fate of the Story* does not have specific Korean references, it still reflects Korean sentiments, especially in the group dynamics of the ensemble.

On the page, I have provided numerous notes with explanations of several cultural and historical references. In *Birds Don't Use a Crosswalk*, these include cultural references such as "hangover soup" and "*Oppa*" as well as political references such as The April Revolution and The Gwangju Uprising. In *Oedipus: The Fate of the* Story, a character recites a passage from *Theogony*, a poem by Hesiod, which is included in a note. *The Wind's Desire* contains notes on the terms wild goose daddy, *yeouiudo*, *yoonjungro*, *Jjuggumi*, *soju*, *cheongju*, Hongdae, *patbinhsu*, mandatory military service, the Sampoong Department Store collapse, and Boshingak. I placed thirty notes in *Sound of the Moon*. Their content includes historical characters, historical instruments including *gayageum*, the history of adjoining nations and geographical locations during the Three Kingdoms period, Korean customs, and even the origin of the battle between the Kim clan and the Park clan. These notes are meant to guide the reader towards a fuller understanding of the specific elements that are essential in each play. While many of the references in the notes deserve more space to be fully comprehensible, I deliberately provided only brief information, in part to stay neutral (as much as possible) with some references that might invite different interpretations and in part to encourage the reader to do their own research and draw their own conclusions as necessary.

English language consultant Anne Hamilton contributed a great deal to the translation and annotation by providing dramaturgical notes from the perspective of a native English speaker who does not speak Korean. Her collaboration in the project covered matters including: titles, the balancing out of diction and tone, questions and suggestions to me regarding word choice and phrasing, and the formatting. In addition, one matter of particular value was her opinion of how to present specific Korean materials, history, vocabulary, and phrases in a consistent manner that could be most easily absorbed by English-speaking readers throughout this collection. Hamilton and I also held two meetings with the playwright during our visit to Korea in February 2024, wherein we shared specific questions for the playwright regarding her overall intentions, and also discussed the playwright's vision for the translations. These consultations and meetings were instrumental in refining the language and the annotation in the translations.

An element of distinctive and transcendent appeal in these plays is that the scope and impact of the action is big enough that regardless of one's level of understanding specific references, one can follow the plot and characters, and enjoy an emotional journey. The playwright, English language consultant, and I consider this narrative strength to have the most potential for the collection's appeal outside of Korea. Yet for the fullest appreciation of these stories, especially on stage, it is imperative that the creative team understand the specific Korean elements, and accordingly convey them to the audience. In the case of this collection, both the translator and the English language consultant are also trained, professional dramaturgs. Therefore, we carefully considered the presentation of the material for future productions through a dramaturgical lens, deciding the following: to provide many historical notes; to format cast lists, time and place notation, scene lists, and stage directions in a clear manner that is consistent with Western standards of stage play formatting; to consider the needs of directors, actors, designers, and musicians in translating the multiple uses of music, both sung and played; and to consistently define and notate words and phrases used in the script to facilitate precise comprehension of the material as a basis of future imaginative interpretation. One benefit I envision from productions of these plays in translation is that they will encourage a study and research of Korea for the director, dramaturg, actors, and designers, therefore enriching their expressive capacities. Material for the audience in the form of program notes and the lobby display will be additionally valuable and essential.

But I'm inclined to push my dramaturgical imagination further than the expected function of dramaturgy and consider the innovation a translation can make. Some creative innovation can start with casting. There is an overarching understanding that these plays are written for Korean actors. However, now that this collection of English-language translations is complete, the broader implication is that non-Korean actors can interpret the roles. I can imagine some production implications for utilizing what we call non-traditional casting in the Western theatre. In a production, interpretation is necessary, based on available actors, talents, and visions, and will inevitably occur. In this respect, the potential of this translation lies in not only expanding cultural artistic expressions outward but also in potentially mining the original work from within and opening it up to the numerous levels of richness embedded within it. The kind of inquiries that a production of a translated play invites is what makes theatrical translation immensely vital for the theatre scene that seeks expansion through diversifying its repertoire and expanding its canon.

Walter Byongsok Chon, Translator

# Notes about the Content and Formatting of the Translation

- The four translated plays – *Birds Don't Use a Crosswalk*, *Oedipus: The Fate of the Story*, *Sound of the Moon*, and *The Wind's Desire* – were chosen in consultation between the author and the translator. This collection of four plays includes several genres exploring Korean history, culture, and sentiments, and represents the author's masterful artistic expressions and achievements.

- Each translation includes a title page and information about the premiere production of the play and about the support from the Daesan Foundation as well as other pertinent information.

- This translation follows the original texts' punctuation as much as possible in order to reflect the original language's pacing and the author's intention. At the same time, because this translation is created for publication and production in English-speaking countries, it uses the formatting recommended by the Dramatists Guild of America. Therefore, placements of character, dialogue, and stage direction in the translation are different from those in the original. In addition, when necessary, character descriptions, stage directions, and notes with necessary information have been added to the translation for clarity and for the reader's convenience.

# Bios of Author (Myung-Wha Kim), Translator (Walter Byongsok Chon), English Language Translation Consultant (Anne M. Hamilton)

MYUNG-WHA KIM (Author) is a playwright and director. She made her debut as a playwright with *Birds Don't Use a Crosswalk*, which won the Samsung Literary Award for Best Play in 1997. Her plays include *First Birthday*, *The Wind's Desire*, *Redolence*, and *The End of the Royal Palace Dining Hall*, among others. She has won numerous awards including the Cha Beom-Seok Theater Award, Daesan Literary Award, Dong-A Theater Award, the Grand Prize in the Asahi Shimbun Theatrical Arts Award, and Yeo Seok-Gi Theater Critic Award. She founded Nanhee Theatre Company in 2018, which became The Nanhee in 2020, and took up directing. The Nanhee's productions include *Mimaji!*, *Dionysus Under the Magnolia*, and *Cold Noodles*.

WALTER BYONGSOK CHON (Translator) is a dramaturg, critic, translator, educator, and theatre scholar from South Korea. He is the Associate Professor of Dramaturgy and Theatre Studies at Ithaca College, U.S. During his sabbatical from Fall 2023 to Spring 2023, he was a Visiting Professor at the School of Drama at Korea National University of Arts. He served as dramaturg at the Yale Repertory Theatre, Yale School of Drama, the Eugene O'Neill Theatre Center, the Great Plains Theater Conference, the Hangar Theatre, the Civic Ensemble, and the New York Musical Festival. He is the co-author (with Anne M. Hamilton) of *Dramaturgy: The Basics* (2023), a practical guidebook in Routledge's The Basics series. His writings have appeared in *Theatre Topics*, *Theater*, *Review*, *Praxis*, *The Korean National Theatre Magazine*, *The Korean Theatre Review*, *Asymptote*, *The Mercurian*, *Situations: Cultural Studies in the Asian Context*, the volumes *The Routledge Companion to Dramaturgy* and *Diversity, Inclusion, and Representation in Contemporary Dramaturgy: Case Studies from the Field*, and the online magazine *The Theatre Times*, for which he is serving as a co-managing editor for South Korea. His produced theatrical translations include Sam-Shik Pai's *Inching Towards Yeolha* (Korean to English) and Charles Mee's *True Love* (English to Korean). His Korean translation of "A Manifesto for the Future Stage," developed at MetaLAB (at) Harvard, is published in the 2022 summer issue of *The Korean Theatre Journal*. He received the 2022 Grant for the Translation of Korean Literary Works from the Daesan Foundation (co-recipient: Anne M. Hamilton). With this grant, he has translated four plays by South Korean playwright Myung-Wha Kim into English. He completed the project with English language translation consultant Anne M. Hamilton. He completed a Bogliasco Foundation Fellowship in Spring 2024. He has presented at various conferences, including ALTA, ASTR, ATHE, GSA, LMDA, MATC, NeMLA, and

PTRS. He has taught theatre at Washington University in St. Louis, Yale School of Drama, University of Nebraska Omaha, Vassar College and Korea National University of Arts. Walter received his B.A. in English from Sungkyunkwan University in Korea, M.A. in theatre studies from Washington University in St. Louis, M.F.A. in dramaturgy and dramatic criticism from Yale School of Drama, and D.F.A. from Yale School of Drama.

ANNE M. HAMILTON (English Language Translation Consultant) is a New York City-based freelance dramaturg and the Founder of Hamilton Dramaturgy, an international consultancy. She has completed two Bogliasco Foundation Fellowships (Fall 1998, Spring 2024). She received the 2022 Grant for the Translation of Korean Literary Works from the Daesan Foundation (co-recipient: Walter Byongsok Chon). With this grant, she served as the English language translation consultant and has completed a collection entitled *An English Theatrical Translation of Korean Plays by Myung-Wha Kim*. Anne has dramaturged for Andrei Serban, Michael Mayer, Lynn Nottage, New York Musical Festival, Niegel Smith, Classic Stage Company, Tina Andrews, Celine Song, The Harold Prince Musical Theatre Institute, The New York City Public Library's Schomberg Center for Research in Black Culture, The University of Iowa Playwrights' Workshop, The Bouwerie Lane Theater/The Jean Cocteau Repertory, Circle Rep, Leslie Lee, Andrew Barrett, the Great Plains Theatre Conference, the Genesis Festival at Crossroads Theatre Company, Pasadena Playhouse/Caltech (Mach33), and the Negro Ensemble Company, among others. She is also an award-winning playwright (*Villa Pompei, I Want to Run Away with You – An Absurdist Fable, Who's Andy Warhol?, The Stacy Play – A Love Song – Part I, Another White Shirt, OFEM,* and *The Shoebox*), and serves as a Company Author for Winterlight Productions in Manhattan. She co-authored *Dramaturgy: The Basics* (2023, with Walter Byongsok Chon), a practical guidebook in Routledge's The Basics series, and created Hamilton Dramaturgy's TheatreNow!, an oral history podcast series. Her chapter "Freelance Dramaturgs in the 21st Century: Journalists, Advocates and Collaborators" appears in *The Routledge Companion to Dramaturgy*. She is a Dramaturgy Editor for *The Theatre Times*, a leading online global theatre journal. She received her B.A. in English literature from Drew University, was a Visiting Student at St Catherine's College at the University of Oxford, and earned her M.F.A. in dramaturgy and theatre criticism from Columbia University School of the Arts.

# Birds Don't Use a Crosswalk

새들은 횡단보도로 건너지 않는다

A full-length drama

By Myung-Wha Kim
Translated from Korean into English by Walter Byongsok Chon
English Language Translation Consultant: Anne M. Hamilton

© 2026 by Byongsok Chon
All rights reserved

* The Korean production of *Birds Don't Use a Crosswalk* premiered at Theatre Aroong-Guji in South Korea under the direction of Oh Tae-seok in 1998.

* This play has been translated with official permission from the author. The contract is available upon inquiry.

* The Daesan Foundation awarded a 2022 Grant for the Translation of Korean Literary Works to Walter Byongsok Chon and Anne Hamilton to create *An English Theatrical Translation of Korean Plays by Myung-Wha Kim*. This collection of four plays includes several genres exploring Korean history, culture, and sentiments, thereby enhancing intercultural theatrical exchange. Walter Byongsok Chon is the translator and Anne Hamilton is the English language translation consultant. The collection includes *Birds Don't Use a Crosswalk*, *Oedipus: The Fate of the Story*, *Sound of the Moon*, and *The Wind's Desire*.

* The translator and English language translation consultant were each awarded a Fellowship by the Bogliasco Foundation, and completed Spring 2024 Residencies in Bogliasco, Italy. *An English Theatrical Translation of Korean Plays by Myung-Wha Kim* was created with the support of a Bogliasco Foundation Fellowship.

*Translator's Note with regards to *Waiting for Godot* in *Birds Don't Use a Crosswalk*: In *Birds Don't Use a Crosswalk*, the theatre club is rehearsing *Waiting for Godot*. While the characters are not quoting the play directly, they enact scenes from it and refer to the play's motif. To include lines from *Waiting for Godot* in a production of *Birds Don't Use a Crosswalk*, copyright must be cleared with the Samuel Beckett estate and official permission must be granted.

Walter Byongsok Chon
© 2026 by Byongsok Chon
All rights reserved

# Characters

| | |
|---|---|
| **Ji-Hwan** | *Male, thirties, Ph.D. student, theatre director.* |
| **Hyun-Woo** | *Male, twenties, college student.* |
| **Joo-Hee** | *Female, twenties, a ghost.* |
| **Girl** | *Female, twenties.* |
| **Mi-Sun** | *Female, twenties, college student.* |
| **Jae-Ho** | *Male, twenties, college student.* |
| **Sung-Tae** | *Male, twenties, college student.* |
| **Hee-Soo** | *Male, twenties, gay, college student.* |
| **Shin-Ae** | *Female, twenties, college student.* |
| **Seung-Jae** | *Male, twenties, Ji-Hwan's college friend, and later 30s, theatre director.* |
| **Min-Soo** | *Male, twenties, Ji-Hwan's college friend.* |
| **Gyu-Tae** | *Male, twenties, Ji-Hwan's college friend.* |
| **Eun-Jung** | *Female, twenties, Ji-Hwan's college friend.* |
| **Jung-Ran** | *Female, twenties, college student.* |
| **Broadcaster** *(in voiceover)* | |
| **Club Promoter** | |
| **Bartender** | |
| **Man One, Two, Three, Four, Five** | |
| **Woman One, Two** | |
| **Middle-Aged Man** | |
| **Metal-Pipe Man One, Two** | |

# Time and Place

Present, Past
Home, Club, Rehearsal Room, Hospital, Night Street, Bar

# Scenes

1. Prologue
2. Ji-Hwan's Home and Club
3. Rehearsal Room/Past
4. Rehearsal Room/Present
5. Rehearsal Room
6. Hospital Room
7. Night Street and Bar
8. Dream and Bar
9. Rehearsal Room/Day
10. Rehearsal Room/Night

## Notes on the Text

* The translation follows the original text's punctuation as much as possible in order to reflect the original language's pacing and the author's intention. The ellipses ".......", "...", and "–" appear in the Korean text.

> Note: In Western script notation, the playwright's use of "......" can be interpreted as being similar to a (*Pause.*).
> Accordingly, "..." is similar to a (*Beat.*).
> And "–" is similar to a breath.

* Notes provide explanations of specific Korean references for the reader's convenience.
* This play contains songs. The lyrics appear in the script. For a production, new music needs to be composed for the songs.

## Content Warning

*This play contains reference to corporal punishment as an element of Korean history and culture.*

*This play contains drinking, smoking, swearing, physical violence, erotic dancing, sex work, and nudity.*

## Scene One: Prologue

*Dark. Noise from the street.*

*Sound of cars.*

*Sound of a sudden stop. Sounds of more sudden stops.*

*Sound of a multiple-vehicle collision.*

*Silence.*

## Scene Two

Setting: **Ji-Hwan**'s Home and Club.

**Ji-Hwan** *is reading a book. There is a window at the back of the stage.*

**Ji-Hwan**    "Society cannot share a common communication system so long as it is split into warring classes. Thus for art to be 'unpolitical' means only to ally itself with the 'ruling' group." . . . "Thus for art to be 'unpolitical'"[1] . . .

*He throws the book aside, stands up, and hovers about. He picks up the TV remote from the couch and turns on the television. Rappers are performing on the television.*

Shit!

*He almost turns off the television but does not.*

Which side are you on? Unpolitical? That means you are criminals of history. But you look too excited for criminals. Is that your punishment? Screaming like a lunatic until the end of time?

*He tries to hum along after them.*

Hey, guys, it's too fast to keep up. I can't understand a damn thing.

*He tries the dance this time and then raps to the beat of the passage he just read.*

"Society cannot share a co-co-co-common communication system so long as it is split into warring classes. Thus for art to be 'unpo-po-po-political'" –

*The phone rings.*

*The set for the Club lights up across the stage from* **Ji-Hwan**'s *room. The silhouette of* **Hyun-Woo** *on his cell phone in the corner appears among silhouettes of people dancing in the dark.* **Hyun-Woo** *is covering his ears because of the club noise.*

**Ji-Hwan**    This is Seo Ji-Hwan . . . Hello.

**Hyun-Woo**    Hello, this is Nahm Hyun-Woo.

**Ji-Hwan**    . . . Who?

**Hyun-Woo**   Nahm Hyun-Woo. I'm the director of the theatre club. Seung-Jae gave me your number.

**Ji-Hwan**   You don't have to shout. I can hear you.

**Hyun-Woo**   You know Seung-Jae, class of '88, right?

**Ji-Hwan**   What's this about?

**Hyun-Woo**   We need your help, please.

**Ji-Hwan**   I said, don't shout.

**Hyun-Woo**   What was that? I can't hear you.

**Ji-Hwan** (*shouting*)   I'm going deaf! So don't shout.

**Hyun-Woo**   I'm so sorry. It's too loud in here.

**Ji-Hwan**   That's your problem. It's quiet here.

**Hyun-Woo**   What was that? I can't hear you. Can you speak up?

**Ji-Hwan**   Damn, man. (*Shouting.*) What do you want from me?

**Hyun-Woo**   Help us, please. We need a director for our fall production.

**Ji-Hwan**   Where the hell is this coming from? Get lost, man. I'm busy.

**Hyun-Woo**   Please, this is urgent. Director Seung-Jae had a car accident. Please help us.

**Ji-Hwan**   I'm done with theatre. And extra-done with the theatre club.

**Voice** (*offstage*)

(*Faintly.*) Ji-Hwan.

**Ji-Whan** *freezes.*

**Voice** (*offstage*)   Ji-Hwan.

**Ji-Hwan**   Who's there?

*Ghastly, strange faces appear in the window. They look worn out and exhausted.*

*They call, "Ji-Hwan."*

**Voice** (*offstage*)   Ji-Hwan –

**Hyun-Woo**   I'm the director of the theatre club! Nahm Hyun-Woo.

**Ji-Hwan**   . . . Go away. This is a dream. Don't do this to me.

**Hyun-Woo**   I have to. This is an emergency.

**Voice** (*offstage*)   Ji-Hwan, aren't you gonna do the show?

**Ji-Hwan** (*to the* **Voice**)   The show?

**Hyun-Woo**   Yes, you'll do it, right? We reserved the space and got the permission and everything, and we can't quit now.

**Voice** (*offstage*)   The barricade's down. The show can't go on.

**Ji-Hwan**   Still, the show must go on. What about the audience?

*The worn-out faces disappear, and there is the image of fire.*

**Hyun-Woo**   Absolutely, the show must still go on.

**Ji-Hwan** (*to the* **Voice**)   . . . Joo-Hee!

**Hyun-Woo**   It's Hyun-Woo. Then I'll take it that you said yes. Thank you. (*He hangs up the phone.*)

**Ji-Hwan** (*snapping back into reality*)   Hey, Hyun-Woo, don't hang up! Hyun-Woo! Damn!

*He throws down the phone and throws himself on the couch.*

*The television screen keeps showing images of the music program.*

**Ji-Hwan**'s *room gets dark, and the Club lights rise.*

*A* **Girl** *with hair dyed a dramatic shade of blonde approaches* **Hyun-Woo**.

**Girl**   Let me use your phone. (*She takes his phone.*)

**Hyun-Woo**   I have to get back to my friends.

**Girl**   Just one call, that's all.

**Hyun-Woo**   An urgent call? To your boyfriend?

**Girl**   Who else would I call at this hour?

**Hyun-Woo**   You ran out of money?

**Girl**   If so, will you lend me some?

**Hyun-Woo**   I can lend you some. Or even pay for your drink.

**Girl**   And the hotel?

**Hyun-Woo**   Phone, drink, and hotel? What am *I* getting?

**Girl** (*putting* **Hyun-Woo**'s *hand on her body*)   A steamy night with a strange girl in a strange place. How does that sound? Too much for just one call? Just kidding, you moron. Don't run away. I won't bite. (*She dials the phone, giggling.*)

**Hyun-Woo** (*taking his phone back*)   You don't have to. Your drink's on me.

**Girl** (*jokingly taking the phone from him again*)   And the hotel?

**Hyun-Woo** (*taking his phone again.*)   And the hangover soup[2] tomorrow.

**Girl** (*taking the phone again.*)   Today's not the only day.

**Mi-Sun** *and* **Jae-Ho** *approach.*

**Mi-Sun**   Who's that?

**Hyun-Woo**   Don't know. She needed to make a call.

**Jae-Ho**   Did you get him? Is he doing it?

**Hyun-Woo**   I think he might, but we'll see.

**Mi-Sun**   I don't like his directing style.

**Hyun-Woo**   We already have our hands full with Sung-Tae. Don't make a fuss over the director and keep your mouth shut.

**Mi-Sun**   Old school directors make a fuss over every little thing. It's so annoying. They yell when you're late. They scold you for wearing short skirts. They scowl at you for being rude –

**Jae-Ho**   They should, I think.

**Girl** (*returning the phone*)   Thanks for this. The guy I'm engaged to is on his way.

**Hyun-Woo**   Tell him not to. I said I got you covered.

**Girl**   My mom told me to act proud when I first meet a man.

**Hyun-Woo**   That's a pity.

**Girl**   There's always a next time. We can do this again.

**Hyun-Woo**   The phone, or the drink?

**Girl**   And everything else. (*She giggles and leaves.*) Bye.

**Jae-Ho**   That's really impressive, man. Hooking up with a girl, just like that.

**Mi-Sun**   Who's that annoying creature? What's your relationship to her? What did you talk about?

**Hyun-Woo**   The guys are waiting. Let's go.

**Jae-Ho**   I'm concerned about Sung-Tae. He might cause trouble.

**Hyun-Woo**   That jerk's always been like that. Let him quit if he wants to.

**Mi-Sun**   I asked you a question. What is your relationship?

**Hyun-Woo**   Hey, leave me alone. You're so irritating.

**Mi-Sun**   *Oppa!*[3]

*Members of the theatre club –* **Sung-Tae***,* **Hee-Soo***,* **Shin-Ae** *– appear, and they all dance sensually.*

*The action switches to* **Ji-Hwan***'s room again.*

**Ji-Hwan** (*dialling his phone*)   Hello. Professor, this is Ji-Hwan. How have you been? (*He turns off the television.*) . . . Yes, that's why I've called. I'm afraid I'll need another semester for my dissertation. I'm sorry. There's something I have to take care of . . . No, this is something personal. I will need some time for this. I need to reorganize my thoughts as well . . . . . . Yes, I'm deeply sorry.

*He hangs up and falls into deep thought.*

Suddenly the earth stops moving. Everything stops, and the clock starts turning backwards. Dark and eerie voices, regretful and yearning voices flow up the River of Forgetfulness. Is this what Hamlet feels when he faces his father's ghost? Completely paralyzed and helplessly dragged along by the ghost's demand? Then is it time for me to draw the sword, like Hamlet does on the spirit's command? Like Orestes does? They wake from a long, long silence. The ghosts, who endured long, cold solitude, are now waiting for me.

*He puts on his coat and lights a cigarette.*

*The action switches to the Club.*

**Sung-Tae**    No way.

**Hyun-Woo**    It's decided.

**Sung-Tae**    We already experienced the 1980s style of directing with Seung-Jae or whatever his name is. And now you want to work with someone he recommended?

**Hyun-Woo**    Don't we have a show to do?

**Hee-Soo**    Let's find another director.

**Hyun-Woo**    The show opens in a month. We don't have time to find another director.

**Hee-Soo**    Is, uhm, is that so?

**Jae-Ho**    We have to think about Seung-Jae's generosity and be grateful. His legs are broken, and he still worries about us.

**Mi-Sun**    Grateful, my ass. When Seung-Jae got into that accident, I remember someone was so relieved that he started singing out loud.

**Jae-Ho**    Do not bring up the past.

**Sung-Tae**    I'm still against it.

**Hyun-Woo**    You want to throw this all away? Everyone else agreed.

**Sung-Tae**    Who agreed? Mi-Sun, Hee-Soo, and my cohort are all against it.

**Jae-Ho**    What's the reason?

**Sung-Tae**    Do I need a reason? I hate it. Get it? I'm sick of the OBs[4] from the 80s.

**Hyun-Woo**    Goddamnit!

(*He kicks the table.*)

**Shin-Ae**    You don't have to get upset. Don't you also hate working with a director you don't get along with? Rather than suffering under a director who's like a dictator, let's cancel the show.

**All**  . . . . . .

**Hee-Soo**  I'm, uhm, fine with that.

**Hyun-Woo**  That's a death wish for all of us. Whenever we have a show, the OBs gather like a pack of dogs and make a mess and impose their military mindset on us like mad men. If we cancel the show, they'll kick our asses real good.

**Shin-Ae**  Then let's cut ties with them completely.

**Jae-Ho**  Hey, you're going to burn down the house to kill some mice? I put all of my part-time job earnings into the production budget, so why should we cancel the show? I can't.

**Sung-Tae**  I did that, too. My whole body yearns for the stage.

**Hyun-Woo**  So let's give this director a chance. If he is not for us, I'll be the one to let him know.

**Mi-Sun**  Once we meet, it's a done deal. When he yells at us with fire in his eyes, can you say, "I don't like you" or "I'm not working with you?"

**Shin-Ae**  Oh, those OB brutes. They'll leave no stone unturned with their criticism.

**Mi-Sun**  "You're rude, you don't get it, you don't think." Ugh –

**Hee-Soo**  "Do this, do that. Don't do this, don't do that."

**Jae-Ho**  "You're all lacking in discipline. Shut up and listen!"

**Hyun-Woo**  "Do you want a beating?"

**All**  "One by one, assume the position." (*They all laugh.*)

**Shin-Ae**  Let's just dance. (*She drags* **Jae-Ho** *to the stage.*)

**Jae-Ho**  Sure, let's just dance. What else is there for us to do? Only dancing cools us down. The generations of the April Revolution[5] and the Gwangju Uprising[6] had it good. They could rally on the street and release their anger. What about us millennials, who are still getting stressed by those hot-blooded OB revolutionaries? What are *we* fighting with? With song and dance!

*Suddenly* **Sung-Tae** *grabs* **Jae-Ho** *by the throat, and the friends try to stop him.*

**Shin-Ae**  What's wrong with him? Is he drunk?

**Hyun-Woo** (*slapping* **Sung-Tae**)  He may be friendly, but he's still an upperclassman to you. How dare you grab him like that?

**Hee-Soo**  Don't use violence. Not you, too. Did Seung-Jae rub off on you?

**Hyun-Woo**  Then should I kiss the bastard who grabs an upperclassman by the throat? There is seriously no discipline here.

**Sung-Tae**  You're just like an army man . . . I'm sorry, Jae-Ho. I'll get going. (*Exits.*)

**Jae-Ho**    Hey, Sung-Tae. (*To* **Hyun-Woo**.) You didn't have to hit him. He was just drunk.

**Hyun-Woo** (*to* **Jae-Ho**)    You should demand respect from these young ones. The kids walk all over you. So rude.

**Hee-Soo**    I'll go check on Sung-Tae.

**Hyun-Woo** (*prevents* **Hee-Soo** *from leaving*)    Let him go. It's better to be hard on him now. If we let him do what he wants, it will be worse once rehearsal starts.

**Jae-Ho**    You're like Machiavelli.

**Shin-Ae**    Let's stop fighting and start dancing. We paid for this.

**Mi-Sun**    Right, go if you will. I'm gonna dance. (*She pulls* **Hyun-Woo** *to the dance floor.*)

*Displeased,* **Hee-Soo** *lights a cigarette, picks up his bag, and leaves.*

*As* **Hee-Soo** *exits, so does* **Ji-Hwan**.

*Loud music and the dancing crowd fill the dance floor.*

*The dancing elevates.*

*Blackout.*


**Scene Three**

Setting: Rehearsal Room/Past.

*The rehearsal room of a university's theatre club. A door opens in the dark.* **Ji-Hwan** *is revealed standing in the doorway. He steps into the rehearsal room. At first he feels strange and awkward, but soon he acclimates himself, and comfortably walks around the stage checking every nook and corner.*

**Ji-Hwan**    It's exactly the same. This musty smell. Pulling you down like a swamp. I would get lost in the script, and then I would look around, and it's like there were creatures crawling around the floor. Like my body was absorbing Estragon and Orestes in the piercing smell. (*He breathes in the air and looks around.*) Still the same. Cigarette butts, liquor bottles, dirty ramen bowls, posters . . . props and stuff.

*Noise from wild animals and birds on the roof.* **Ji-Hwan** *looks up at the roof with nostalgia.*

On the roof.

**Joo-Heew** (*offstage, in the dark*)    On the roof –

**Ji-Hwan**    On the roof are doves.

**Joo-Hee** (*offstage*)    On the roof are doves –

**Ji-Hwan**   . . . Who's there?

**Joo-Hee** (*offstage*)   . . . . . .

**Ji-Hwan**   Who's there?

**Joo-Hee** (*offstage, laughs*)

**Ji-Hwan**   That voice.

**Joo-Hee** (*emerging from the dark*)   On the roof, doves are clattering. The sound Ji-Hwan used to like.

**Ji-Hwan**   Joo-Hee.

**Joo-Hee**   Yes, it's me.

**Ji-Hwan**   . . . I haven't thought about you in a long time, yet there you are.

**Joo-Hee**   There *you* are. I've always been here.

**Ji-Hwan**   Always?

**Joo-Hee**   Always waiting for you.

**Ji-Hwan**   . . . I missed you.

**Joo-Hee** (*walking around* **Ji-Hwan**)   You're all grown up. Wearing a Burberry coat like a middle-aged man, showing lines on your forehead like someone with a stomach disease. Have you had no laughs all this time? Has your whole life been miserable?

**Ji-Hwan**   I missed you.

**Joo-Hee**   I know. We all missed you, too.

**Ji-Hwan**   We?

**Joo-Hee**   Yes, we. Hey, everyone! Ji-Hwan is back. Ji-Hwan is back in the theatre club.

*She takes out a whistle from her pocket and, as she blows it, the curtains are drawn, the cabinets are opened, and the tablecloths are flipped.* **Ji-Hwan**'s *old friends appear, making firebombs and demonstration posters. They are* **Seung-Jae**, **Min-Soo**, **Gyu-Tae**, *and* **Eun-Jung**. *They move like a squeaking music box doll that's not oiled or whose battery has run out. Their speech is heavy and fragmented, like a slow, rusty machine. But they should possess a poignancy which transcends that of everyday life, and also a unique lyricism, evoking nostalgia like a black and white photo. Like an old song from an antique gramophone.*

**Seung-Jae**   Hi. Last night I –

**Joo-Hee/Min-Soo/Gyu-Tae/Eun-Jung**   Last night?

**Seung-Jae**   dreamt I was running away.

**Joo-Hee/Min-Soo/Gyu-Tae/Eun-Jung**   Oh! A dream.

**Seung-Jae**   I heard footsteps.

**Joo-Hee/Min-Soo/Gyu-Tae/Eun-Jung**   Footsteps?

**Seung-Jae**   When I look back, I see nothing, but the footsteps get closer.

**Joo-Hee/Min-Soo/Gyu-Tae/Eun-Jung**   *Thump thump – Thump thump –*

**Seung-Jae**   I'm afraid they'll catch me soon.

**Joo-Hee/Min-Soo/Gyu-Tae/Eun-Jung**   Oh! That again.

**Seung-Jae**   Will we see the world we believe in?

**Min-Soo**   Of course we will.

**Joo-Hee/Min-Soo/Gyu-Tae/Eun-Jung**   Really?

**Min-Soo**   Really.

**Seung-Jae**   When?

**Gyu-Tae**   Someday. We have to believe.

**Joo-Hee/Min-Soo/Gyu-Tae/Eun-Jung**   Someday. We believe.

**Seung-Jae**   Will we see it in our lifetime?

**Joo-Hee/Min-Soo/Gyu-Tae/Eun-Jung**   Will we?

**Gyu-Tae**   If we fight for it, we certainly will.

**Joo-Hee/Min-Soo/Gyu-Tae/Eun-Jung**   If we fight for it, we will, soon.

**Joo-Hee**   If we fight for it? . . . . . . If we fight for it.

**Ji-Hwan**   Min-Soo. Seung-Jae. Eun-Jung . . . Gyu-Tae . . . You've been here all along . . . I forgot about this, about everything, . . . I'm back. I'm here. It's Ji-Hwan.

*Everybody notices* **Ji-Hwan**.

*Their movement and speech become normal and full strength, like that of a newly charged tape recorder.*

**Gyu-Tae**   You traitor.

**Min-Soo**   Why didn't you come to the gathering? And the study group?

**Eun-Jung**   Some of our friends are working at factories instead of going to college.

**Seung-Jae**   A friend lost his vision from a firebomb. My friends are getting hurt. They're dying.

**Gyu-Tae**   Yet you are reading the *Poetics* in the library. How can you focus on the *Poetics*?

**Ji-Hwan**   Yes, I did that. I remember Gyu-Tae snatching away my *Poetics*. But that's all in the past, and what you say doesn't bother me anymore. (*He says his lines like he's chanting a spell.*) I'm not angry. I'm not angry.

**Eun-Jung**   This is no time to study for the test. Close your book.

**Seung-Jae**   Don't hesitate. We don't have time.

**Min-Soo**   5pm today. In front of Myeongdong Cathedral.[7]

**Ji-Hwan**   No more fights. Nobody fights anymore.

**Gyu-Tae**   Skeptical coward. It's because of cowards like you that the world doesn't change.

**Ji-Hwan** (*shaking his head*)   I'm not angry. I'm not angry.

**Gyu-Tae**   Is your body so precious, you worthless opportunist? You're not even an intellectual.

**Ji-Hwan**   Ahhh!

*He jumps on* **Gyu-Tae***.*

*Everyone shouts and gathers around* **Ji-Hwan** *and* **Gyu-Tae***, who are fighting. It resembles a dogfight.*

**All** (*chant*)
  Fight, fight!.
  We got action.
  We got fight.
  Free the proletariat.
  Down with dictatorship.
  Hurrah for democracy.
  Comrades, unite.
  Enemies, stand down.

**Joo-Hee** *abruptly blows the whistle. Everyone stops moving.*

**Min-Soo** (*to* **Ji-Hwan**)   Are you a comrade or an enemy?

**Ji-Hwan**   I'm not your enemy.

**Gyu-Tae**   You are not our comrade. (*He jumps on top of* **Ji-Hwan**.)

**All** (*chant*)
  Fight, fight!
  Fight with more intensity.
  Fight more relentlessly.
  For the freedom of the people! March forward.
  All we've got is fight, fight –
  Fight, or be defeated.
  Punch, punch. Left and right.
  Join us, comrades, and unite.

**Joo-Hee** *blows the whistle.*

**Seung-Jae**   What made you come back?

**Ji-Hwan** (*out of breath*)   I want to make theatre. That's why I came back.

**All** . . . . . .

**Eun-Jung**    Theatre?

**Ji-Hwan**    Yes, make theatre like I used to.

**Gyu-Tae**    Like you used to?

**Joo-Hee/Min-Soo/Seung-Jae/Eun-Jung**    Like you used to? . . . Like you used to?

*The set changes. The lights change, and a three-colored flag, representing the French flag, comes down from the ceiling.* **Seung-Jae** *is standing under the flag.*

**Seung-Jae**    "I pose this question to you. Should several hundred corpses stand in our way as we complete the final stages of our revolution? When Moses led his people across the Red Sea and the wilderness, the old and corrupt generation had to be wiped out, before he could build a new nation. Legislators! We don't have the Red Sea or the wilderness, but we have the war and the guillotine. A revolution is like the daughters of Pelias: they tear humanity apart so that they can rejuvenate it. Humanity will rise up from the crucible of blood, like the earth rises from the waves of the flood with primal limbs, as if it was its first creation."[8]

**Joo-Hee/Min-Soo/Gyu-Tae/Eun-Jung**
        Bravo, Hurrah, Saint-Just,
        Hurrah, French Revolution,
        A revolution feeds on blood.
        Aristocrats to the guillotine!
        Bourgeoisie to the guillotine!
        Hurrah, Proletariat!

**Min-Soo** (*quietly*)    Ji-Hwan, it's your turn. You're okay? Say your line!

**Ji-Hwan**    . . . That play was a misinterpretation!

**All** . . . . . .

**Ji-Hwan**    Changing the hero from Danton to Saint-Just and Robespierre was not necessary.

**Gyu-Tae**    Danton is a skeptic. He's skeptical of the revolution.

**Ji-Hwan**    Yes, he's a skeptic. Is that wrong? Having doubts means having self-reflection. Not having self-reflection leads to dogmatism. I'm more afraid of people who don't doubt themselves. They only see what they want to see.

**Gyu-Tae**    Then do you doubt that the proletariat is being exploited by the military and the conglomerates? Do you doubt the revolution?

**Ji-Hwan**    I'm talking about the method . . . I'm talking about Danton.

**Gyu-Tae**    What counts is the goal. A proletarian revolution, by all means possible. We don't have time to doubt our method.

**Ji-Hwan**    We could be wrong. There could be other ways to accomplish this.

**Gyu-Tae**   You are wrong. Not us.

**Ji-Hwan**   Hardliner.

**Gyu-Tae**   . . . Parasite. Pushover.

**Ji-Hwan**   Stubborn fundamentalist.

**Gyu-Tae**   Cunning neutralist.

**Ji-Hwan**   You, are a fascist.

**Gyu-Tae**   Ahhh!

*As* **Gyu-Tae** *grabs* **Ji-Hwan** *by the throat,* **Joo-Hee** *blows the whistle.*

**Eun-Jung**   Why'd you do that? The fight didn't even start.

**Joo-Hee**   There's a change in the air.

**Joo-Hee/Min-Soo/Gyu-Tae/Eun-Jung**   . . . . . . .

**Min-Soo**   The air is toxic!

**Joo-Hee/Min-Soo/Gyu-Tae/Eun-Jung**   The air is toxic. We forgot about this.

*There is a faraway sound of pepper fog spray being dispersed. It gets closer. Everyone, except for* **Ji-Hwan**, *takes a defensive position and steps back little by little.*

**Ji-Hwan**   What's going on, guys?

**Seung-Jae/Joo-Hee/Min-Soo/Gyu-Tae/Eun-Jung**   We forgot about this. We're busy.

**Ji-Hwan**   Where are you all headed?

**Seung-Jae**   I hear them from the east. A lot of 'em. The enemies.

**Eun-Jung**   I smell them from the west. Toxic. Very toxic.

**Ji-Hwan**   Did something happen?

**Min-Soo**   The barricades are down in the south. It's dangerous, very dangerous.

**Gyu-Tae**   The sky is in flames in the north. Big, very big flames.

**Ji-Hwan**   Are you still fighting? . . . Is the fight still going on?

**Seung-Jae/Joo-Hee/Min-Soo/Gyu-Tae/Eun-Jung**   Don't leave the formation. Hold on tight, arm in arm.

**Ji-Hwan**   The play, what about the play?

**Seung-Jae/Joo-Hee/Min-Soo/Gyu-Tae/Eun-Jung**   The play? Oh! Yes, the play.

**Gyu-Tae**   Focus, everyone! It's time to fight! We have to fight the enemy! Now is the time to unite and attack!

**Seung-Jae/Joo-Hee/Min-Soo/Eun-Jung**   Now is the time to unite and attack!

**Ji-Hwan**    Then what about the play? The audience is waiting.

**Seung-Jae/Joo-Hee/Min-Soo/Gyu-Tae/Eun-Jung**    Later, when we have a better world. Ahhh! (*They run out, shouting.*)

**Joo-Hee** *stops, looks at* **Ji-Hwan**, *and runs out.*

**Ji-Hwan**    . . . Joo-Hee, don't go. You can't leave me here.

*Time frame: The present.*

*The friends from the past are all gone, and the rehearsal room returns to what it was upon* **Ji-Hwan***'s entrance. The door opens, and current club members* **Hyun-Woo**, **Mi-Sun**, **Jae-Ho**, *and* **Shin-Ae** *enter. The stage gets bright.*

**Hyun-Woo**    Hello, you must be Ji-Hwan. You're early. Everyone, say hello. This is Ji-Hwan. .

**Everyone**    Hello, nice to meet you.

**Mi-Sun**    . . . He's handsome.

**Ji-Hwan** *looks at the members.*

**Hyun-Woo**    I'm sorry the room is so messy. This is Jae-Ho, who's in my year. This is Shin-Ae and Mi-Sun . . . .

*While* **Hyun-Woo** *busily introduces the members, the stage darkens.*

**Hyun-Woo** (*who is now heard as a voice in the dark*)    There's a few who are not here. They've been causing some trouble. I'll make sure to teach them . . .

*Cheerful music is turned on and buries his voice.*


**Scene Four**

Setting: Rehearsal Room/Present.

*The stage lights up, and* **Ji-Hwan** *is sitting at the center, facing downstage. The other members are sitting apart from him, almost surrounding him.*

**Shin-Ae**    Please answer within five seconds.

**Hyun-Woo**    This is just a simple test. Since we don't know anything about you.

**Mi-Sun**    We need to be rational. We can't collaborate with someone who is not compatible.

**Ji-Hwan**    I'm your OB.

**Hee-Soo**    That's the problem.

**Ji-Hwan**    You called *me* for help.

**Sung-Tae**    Why so fussy? You can always quit.

**Ji-Hwan**    . . . Okay. Let's do it. Ask away.

*The inquiry proceeds quickly, like a ping-pong match.* **Ji-Hwan** *sometimes misses a beat, but the others are completely into the fast pace.*

**Shin-Ae**    Are you voting in the fall election?

**Ji-Hwan**    . . . Well.

**Mi-Sun**    How much do you drink?

**Ji-Hwan**    Wait, I wasn't done yet.

**Shin-Ae**    After five seconds, we move on to the next question. Mi-Sun, continue.

**Mi-Sun**    Do you get drunk?

**Ji-Hwan**    Not all the time, but sometimes . . .

**Mi-Sun**    Have you ever gotten so drunk, you broke a bottle to fight?

**Ji-Hwan**    Well . . . a few times, no, several times –

**Mi-Sun**    Do you kick ass, or get your ass kicked?

**Ji-Hwan**    . . . Which do you think?

**Shin-Ae**    You don't ask. You only answer.

**Ji-Hwan**    . . . . . .

**Jae-Ho**    What's unique about Wong Kar Wai films?

**Ji-Hwan**    Fast cinematography, slow dialogue.

**Jae-Ho**    Meaning?

**Ji-Hwan**    The world may spin around you, but you have to take your time.

**Jae-Ho** (*impressed*)    Wow.

**Jung-Ran**    First thing you do on a Sunday morning?

**Ji-Hwan**    I fold the blanket. No, I look at the clock.

**Jung-Ran**    What brand is your toothbrush?

**Ji-Hwan**    Hey, what kind of a question is that? Ask me about something important.

**Jung-Ran**    What. Like metadiscourse?

**Hee-Soo**    Move on. What's your take on the death of Leslie Cheung?

**Ji-Hwan**    Who is Leslie Cheung? . . . Oh, that actor?

**Jung-Ran**    Do you eat rice or bread for breakfast?

**Ji-Hwan** *smirks.*

**Jung-Ran**    You keep smirking. (*She addresses the others.*) He ignores the importance of the everyday. (*There is light booing from everyone.*)

**Mi-Sun**   Why are you still single? What do you think about chastity before marriage?

**Ji-Hwan**   Hold! Stop! What's the rush? Give me some time. Do you want my answer or not?

**Shin-Ae**   Answer in five seconds, that's the rule.

**Ji-Hwan**   How can I answer when you're barraging me with questions?

**Shin-Ae**   That's the point. We want to learn who you really are, not what you think or what you contrive. Not the complicated, fabricated, contrived image of you, but the real you.

**Ji-Hwan**   Really? . . . Okay. Keep going. (**Ji-Hwan** *answers, from now on becoming more casual and nonchalant.*)

**Hee-Soo**   Sing the latest hit song by the group H.O.T.

**Ji-Hwan**   I don't know any current hits.

**Sung-Tae**   What are three signature songs by the band Uhuhboo Project?[9]

**Ji-Hwan**   Who? Uh-huh-what?

**Jae-Ho**   Let's pass. Three snacks that go well with beer?

**Hyun-Woo**   He hates questions like that.

**Sung-Tae**   What's wrong with them? You can tell a person by what he likes to eat.

**Ji-Hwan**   Squid, potatoes, tofu stew.

**Shin-Ae**   Jae-Ho. Analysis.

**Jae-Ho**   His taste is folksy, and tofu stew signifies a simple and well-rounded character.

**Jung-Ran**   Tofu stew with beer . . . Isn't that tacky?

**Mi-Sun**   You're no good, Jae-Ho. Stay out of it. Are you in love?

**Ji-Hwan**   I'm not answering that.

**Mi-Sun**   When did you lose your virginity?

**Ji-Hwan** (*sighs*)   My gap year. Wanna know where?

**Shin-Ae**   Answers only.

**Hee-Soo**   Are you for or against homosexuality?

**Ji-Hwan**   For.

**Hee-Soo**   If your brother was gay, what would you do?

**Ji-Hwan**   I would accept him.

**Sung-Tae**   What if a guy who likes you wants to kiss you?

**Ji-Hwan**   I would say go for it.

**Sung-Tae**  How about me, now? (*Gets up.*)

**Ji-Hwan** (*startled*)   What's wrong with you? . . . Don't test me!

**Sung-Tae**   See that? He hasn't been truthful.

**Shin-Ae**   Ji-Hwan. We want the truth from you. Don't just throw out an answer or kid around, please. It's offensive, like you're treating us like children.

**Ji-Hwan** (*sighs*)   Are you done?

**Hee-Soo**   Are you for or against homosexuality?

**Ji-Hwan**   Are you gay? Why do you keep asking that?

**Hee-Soo**   . . . . . . Yes.

**Ji-Hwan**   I'm sorry?

**Hee-Soo**   I'm ga—, gay. So please be honest.

**Ji-Hwan**   . . . Against.

**Hee-Soo**   Why?

**Ji-Hwan**   It feels weird.

**Hee-Soo**   Did, did you hear that? I can't accept him. Absolutely not.

**Hyun-Woo**   Hee-Soo!

**Hee-Soo**   Do—, don't pressure me. I me—, mean what I sa—, say.

**Sung-Tae**   I'm also against this old-timer directing our show.

**Jae-Ho**   I'd say yes. He likes tofu stew, so let's give him a chance.

**Hyun-Woo**   Me, too.

**Sung-Tae**   You're the club president, so of course you're a yes. How about you, Shin-Ae?

**Shin-Ae**   Abstain.

**Hyun-Woo**   Shin-Ae Kang. You're a senior. Don't you feel responsible?

**Shin-Ae**   I can't figure him out.

**Hee-Soo**   It looks like we have a verdict. (**Hee-Soo** *counts the hands.*) No for Mi-Sun, obviously.

**Mi-Sun**   I'm a yes.

**All**   What?

**Mi-Sun**   Yes. I like him. I'd like to work with him.

**All** *look at* **Mi-Sun** *with confusion.*

**Ji-Whan**   What's the verdict?

**Hyun-Woo**  Congratulations. You have a tough road ahead of you.

**Ji-Hwan** (*gently*)  So there's no turning back from this?

**Hyun-Woo**  No.

**Ji-Hwan**  No one's dropping out no matter what?

**Hyun-Woo**  Of course.

**Ji-Whan**  Promise?

**Jae-Ho**  You got it.

**Ji-Hwan**  Everyone agrees?

**Jae-Ho**  Of course. We accept the verdict.

**Ji-Hwan**  So I can trust you all?

**Jae-Ho/Hyun-Woo** (*together*)  Yes. (*They urge everyone else to say yes.*)

**Ji-Hwan**  Alright, you sorry lots. I'm gonna teach you a good lesson today. What was all that about? You call me up here and have the audacity to test me?

*He gets up and urges everyone to move downstage. Now it looks like* **Ji-Hwan** *is standing above them.*

You, with the ponytail. Stop staring and sit down. You hear me? Listen up. I'll make sure to correct your insubordinate attitude through this process. Is that clear? Good. We'll have a brief test. Shoot out the answer rapidly. Within five seconds. You. Who is Moon Ik-Hwan?

**Jung-Ran**  Who? . . . A wo—, worker?

**Ji-Hwan**  If you don't know, say you don't know. Anyone been to Mangweol-Dong? . . . Of course not. Top three appetizers for *soju*?

**Jae-Ho**  Potato stew, scallion pancake, and pork feet.

**Ji-Hwan**  You must be all rich. Bastards. Back in my day, a plate of blood sausage with shrimp crackers was a luxury.

**Sung-Tae**  And you're proud of that?

**Ji-Hwan**  You, mumbler. What's the true spirit of rock?

**Sung-Tae**  . . . Alternative.

**Ji-Hwan**  What's that?

**Sung-Tae**  A. L. T. E. R. N. A. T. I. V. E. to spell it out. A substitute of sort. (*The others giggle.*)

**Ji-Hwan**  Give me more.

**Sung-Tae**  Dreaming of a different world.

**Ji-Hwan**    You must know that, without this world, there cannot be a different world.

**Sung-Tae**    Fuck me, I've had enough. Just stick to directing, man. We don't need a teacher.

**Hyun-Woo** (*elbows* **Sung-Tae**)    Shut up. I'm sorry, Ji-Hwan. He's a bit aggressive.

**Ji-Hwan**    The absence of discipline here is appalling. Do you want to see what real discipline looks like?

**Shin-Ae**    Is the objective of this test to discipline us?

**Ji-Hwan**    . . . What's your take on sex before marriage? Is anyone still a virgin?

**Mi-Sun**    You can check it yourself. How about tonight? I am free.

**Ji-Hwan** (*laughs*)    Okay, last question. What kind of theatre do you want to make?

**Jae-Ho**    Theatre that's emotional, not rational.

**Mi-Sun**    Something sensual.

**Jung-Ran**    Something light and ordinary, not heavy and serious.

**Shin-Ae**    A theatre that expresses an authentic self, rather than a hypocritical historical perspective. What kind of theatre do *you* want to make?

**Ji-Hwan**    You just answer. You're not qualified to ask questions. Anyone else? You, the gay one. What kind of theatre do you want to make?

**Hee-Soo**    . . . a theatre for marginalized identities. A theatre that criticizes people who have fixed ideas about what's normal and what's not, and that embraces marginalized identities for who they are.

**Ji-Hwan**    . . . Good. That's it for the test. Congratulations on passing it with excellence! Following in Seung-Jae's footsteps, I will be directing your production. Let's work together democratically!

**Shin-Ae**    We called you up here to simply get to know you. But you tried to dominate us as soon as you walked in the door. Would a democratic process be even possible?

**Ji-Hwan**    If you lack the most basic common sense, this is as democratic as it can get for you. Learn some manners before you argue.

**Sung-Tae**    I'd rather quit this theatre club than work with this creature.

**Ji-Hwan**    Nobody leaves until this production is over. You just promised. We're all in this together till it's done. Right? . . . Let's go outside and warm up our vocals. (*He exits with a smile.*)

**Sung-Tae**    . . . I'll break his skull if he mentions discipline one more time.

**Jae-Ho**    Stop talking nonsense and watch your own skull.

**Shin-Ae**    We're in big trouble, right? We dodged the wolf but ended up with a tiger.

**Hee-Soo** *kicks the chair in front of him and exits.*

**Hyun-Woo**    This doesn't bode well for me.

**Mi-Sun**    I like him. He's cool. Charismatic and smart.

**All**    . . . . . .

*Blackout.*


**Scene Five**

Setting: Rehearsal Room.

*It is still dark. Only* **Ji-Hwan**'s *voice is heard.*

**Ji-Hwan**    It's pitch black. You can't see anything. The only sounds are the creaking of the chairs and the rustling made by your movements. In the dark, the world outside slowly fades, and people hold their breath waiting for a new world. Now, just like the light at the beginning of time, the stage lights up. And . . . . . . the play begins.

*A dim light hits the stage.*

*A tree faintly appears, with* **Jae-Ho** *sitting under it.*

**Ji-Hwan**    Light hits the stage, and there is a tree. A bare tree, with no fruit, no leaf . . . No, the light's coming too quickly. That's not dramatic. More slowly . . . Good. Lighting, remember this. That's the right speed . . . Now, the world around the tree slowly emerges. There's nothing there. It's lonely and desolate and quiet. Like it's the end of the world. In that bleak landscape sits Gogo, old, tired, and grumpy. Jae-Ho, remember this brightness. Once the stage is fully lit . . . Go.

**Jae-Ho** (*as Estragon*) *tries to take off his boot but fails. He tries again and falls.*

**Hee-Soo** (*as Vladimir*) *enters with the script and says Didi's first line.*

**Ji-Hwan**    Not yet. You enter *after* Jae-Ho's line. (**Hee-Soo** *exits.*)

**Jae-Ho** (*as Estragon*) *tries to take off his boot but fails. He says Gogo's first line.*

**Ji-Hwan**    Aren't you entering?

**Hee-Soo** (*as Vladimir*) *enters running.*

**Ji-Hwan**    You can't run. You take your time. Jae-Ho. From the top.

**Jae-Ho** (*as Estragon*) *says his first line. As* **Hee-Soo** *does not enter, he repeats his line.*

**Hee-Soo** (*as Vladimir*) *enters slowly.*

**Ji-Hwan**    Why are you so late?

**Hee-Soo**    You said take your time.

**Ji-Hwan**    You still need to get the timing right.

**Hee-Soo**    Don't be so hard on me. I'm an understudy anyway. Am I expected to get everything right?

**Ji-Hwan**    . . . Okay. Continue.

**Hee-Soo** (*as Vladimir*) *reads several of Didi's lines without pausing.*

**Ji-Hwan**    Hey! You need to commit yourself even as an understudy. If you throw away your lines like that, how can Jae-Ho catch up with you? Again, pervert.

**Hee-Soo**    . . . . . .

**Ji-Hwan**    Say your line.

**Hee-Soo** (*as Vladimir*) *stutters this time.*

**Ji-Hwan**    Are you kidding me? (*He jumps up from the auditorium and smacks* **Hee-Soo.**)

**Hee-Soo**    What —, what the hell, man!

**Ji-Hwan**    Are you acting out for being an understudy? Why are you stuttering all of a sudden?

**Jae-Ho**    That's how he is.

**Ji-Hwan**    What?

**Jae-Ho**    He stutters from time to time. He's fine usually, but when he speaks in public or when he's cornered, he stutters.

**Ji-Hwan** (*sighs*)    I'm sorry.

**Hee-Soo**    That—, that's alright.

**Ji-Hwan**    Let's continue.

**Hee-Soo** (*as Vladimir*) *tries saying his lines, still stuttering.*

I can't do this.

**Ji-Hwan**    It's alright. You're doing fine.

**Hee-Soo**    Ple—, please use someone else. I get so nerv—, nervous in front of people . . . I've ne—, never acted before.

**Jae-Ho**    Hee-Soo really has never acted before. He got a part in freshman year, but the director cut him because he couldn't handle it.

**Ji-Hwan**    . . . Why is Sung-Tae late today?

**Jae-Ho**    I didn't hear from him.

**Ji-Hwan**    What is wrong with you all? Our opening is right around the corner. And the lead is late, and the understudy is –

**Sung-Tae** (*enters, carrying a motorcycle helmet*)    Sorry I'm late.

**Ji-Hwan** *kicks* **Sung-Tae** *on the shin, and* **Sung-Tae***, in pain, holds his leg and hops around the stage.*

**Ji-Hwan**    Get ready.

**Sung-Tae**    This is a complete dictatorship.

**Ji-Hwan**    Don't give me any excuses. Stop complaining and get ready.

**Sung-Tae**    I can explain.

**Ji-Hwan**    You could have called. You have a cell phone, right?

**Sung-Tae**    Some things are just unavoidable.

**Ji-Hwan**    You doing this on your own? We can't rehearse without you.

**Sung-Tae**    For fuck's sake, I said I was sorry!

**Ji-Hwan** *breathes deeply in frustration.*

**Jae-Ho** (*carefully*)    Hey, Sung-Tae, let's rehearse, okay?

**Hee-Soo** (*puts the costume hat on* **Sung-Tae** *and drags him on to the stage*)    Yes, Sung-Tae. Come on.

**Jae-Ho** (*as Estragon*) *gets into character and falls down with his boot in his hands. However, there is no reaction from* **Sung-Tae***.*

**Ji-Hwan**    Seung-Jae told me what a handful you guys are, but this is beyond what I could ever imagine. Your lack of discipline is just –

**Sung-Tae**    Enough with the discipline. I'm sick of it.

**Hee-Soo**    Sung-Tae. Please.

**Sung-Tae**    Am I wrong here? They fought against the military dictatorship, fine, but now they talk discipline to us. *This* is a dictatorship.

**Ji-Hwan**    That's no way to talk to your senior.

**Sung-Tae**    Fuck it, man, this is who I am. What're you gonna do about it?

**Shin-Ae** *and* **Mi-Sun** *enter with a ladle, pot, and a bowl.*

**Shin-Ae**    Ta-da, here we are. Today's special. Made by your chefs Kang Shin-Ae and Park Mi-Sun. All-in-one stew.

*She and* **Mi-Sun** *wave the ladle and spoon in a comic dance and sing.*
  Pick up the spoon
  Pick up the spoon
  First fill your belly
  Then get to work.
  for those who are hungry
  for those who feed the hungry
  pick up the spoon. pick up –

**All**   . . . . . .

**Shin-Ae**   What's going on?

**Sung-Tae** (*to* **Jae-Ho** *who stops him from leaving*)   I told you I was against working with someone who went to school in the '80s. Why did you have to drag me in here?

**Ji-Hwan**   Let that bastard go! He's no good. Get out. The stage doesn't need a brat like you.

**Sung-Tae** *stares for a moment and then exits.*

**Ji-Hwan**   Hee-Soo. You play his part today.

**Hee-Soo**   I can't! Please. I have stage fright. You saw how much I stutter.

**Ji-Hwan**   You're not stuttering now.

**Hee-Soo**   I stu—, stutter when I get ner—, nervous.

**Ji-Hwan**   Is he for real? . . . What a loser. (*He takes out a cigarette and heads out.*)

**Mi-Sun**   Ji-Hwan. What about lunch?

**Ji-Hwan**   Forget about it.

**Mi-Sun**   I put an egg in there, especially for you. I even brought homemade side dishes.

**Ji-Hwan**   Does it look like I'm in the mood? (*Exits.*)

**Mi-Sun**   . . . . . .

**Jae-Ho**   Hey, Mi-Sun. Let's eat.

**Mi-Sun**   Forget about it.

**Shin-Ae**   Try it. It's gourmet, and I made it.

**Mi-Sun**   Does it look like I'm in the mood?

**All**   . . . . . .

*Blackout.*


**Scene Six**

Setting: Hospital Room.

*Cheerful and rhythmic music in the darkness.*

*Noise interferes.*

**Broadcaster** (*in voiceover*)   This is an announcement for the labor union. The hospital and the union committee have entered the fourth round of negotiations.

*The stage lights up, and at center stage are* **Seung-Jae** *in a wheelchair and* **Ji-Hwan**.

*In the background is a faint silhouette of* **Gyu-Tae** *in a patient outfit.*

**Seung-Jae**    The kids are a handful, right?

**Ji-Hwan**    Tell me about it, man. What's wrong with the cast? I scolded the lead because he was late, and he doesn't show up for a whole week. You know, Sung-Tae.

**Seung-Jae**    You shouldn't mess with him. He's like a beehive. You touch him, and he'll be all over you. Still, he's a terrific actor.

**Ji-Hwan**    What good does that do? Riding a motorcycle like he's cool or something. I'm giving his part to Hee-Soo.

**Seung-Jae**    He stutters. And that motorcycle is not for show. Sung-Tae makes a living with it. You know Quick Service delivery? He makes quick deliveries all across the city, through the traffic jams. He's a motorcycle man.

**Ji-Hwan**    Sung-Tae is poor?

**Seung-Jae**    Gyu-Tae went to a mental institution. His single mother –

**Ji-Hwan**    What are you talking about?

**Gyu-Tae** *becomes more visible.*

**Seung-Jae**    Sung-Tae is Gyu-Tae's youngest brother. Didn't you know? I guess his frustration makes him act nasty. Maybe we remind him of his brother. How could we not? . . . You're still holding on to it, right? It's been ten years. It's time to forgive Gyu-Tae. He couldn't stop Joo-Hee from setting herself on fire. You know how she was.

**Ji-Hwan**    Let's not talk about that.

**Seung-Jae**    It's not just Joo-Hee. Everybody went manic back then. We were all willing to risk our lives for our cause.

**Ji-Hwan**    But he did nothing, knowing she was going to die. She was twenty-two . . . I remember clearly the day we buried Joo-Hee. You know what he said at her memorial. That Joo-Hee committed a noble deed. When her corpse was so burnt down it was completely unrecognizable . . . . . .

**Seung-Jae**    Gyu-Tae actually ran after her. But the fire was already all over Joo-Hee. What can you do? I guess that's Joo-Hee's luck. (*Laughs.*) We fought our asses off, and for what? The world is still a mess. In this damn country, all you gotta do is look after yourself. Look at me. Six years of college as an activist, got arrested as a protester, three years in the army, and I have nothing to show for all that. Others are now judges and prosecutors or at least work for a company and own an apartment and a car and fly to Saipan or Hawaii for vacations. *Shoong!*

**Ji-Hwan**    Do you regret it?

**Seung-Jae**    I am full of regrets . . . But the funny things is, my friend. If I go back in time, I might do it all over again. Fuck this bullshit. Fuck this country. What the hell am I saying? Am I violating the National Security Act?

**Ji-Hwan**    Man, you're still a clown. Hey, do you remember?

**Seung-Jae**    ......?

**Ji-Hwan**    When the school banned our performance –

**Seung-Jae**    Stop that, you bastard.

**Ji-Hwan**    We got so drunk and protested in front of the Dean of Student Affairs office in our underwear. (*Laughs.*)

**Seung-Jae**    Yes, and I accidentally stepped on a dog's tail. (*Laughs.*) Don't laugh, you jerk. You ran away and left me alone there.

**Ji-Hwan**    . . . Hey, Seung-Jae. How about we do it together now?

**Seung-Jae**    What?

**Ji-Hwan**    Why don't you start? (*Holds up his fist.*)

**Seung-Jae**    Let's do it together. (*Holds up his fist.*)
       Together
  Rise up sun rise up
  Giving it **all** for the stage
  Rise up sun rise up
  Hit the drum . . . . . . (*They look at each other.*)

**Ji-Hwan**    I gotta go. Take care, man.

**Seung-Jae** *nods.*

**Ji-Hwan** *exits.*

**Broadcaster** (*in voiceover*)    This is an announcement for the labor union. The negotiations came to an impasse.

As of this moment, we are on strike. We repeat. As of this moment, we are on strike.

**Protesters** (*from far away*)    Give us our rights, or give us death!

**Seung-Jae**    Fuck this world –

*Blackout.*


**Scene Seven**

Setting: Night Street and Bar.

*A motorcycle is heard in the dark. The sound of several motorcycles roaming the streets.*

*The stage lights up and shows the front of a seedy bar in a back alley.*

*Near the entrance of the bar, the* **Club Promoter** *is soliciting people.*

*A drunk person is throwing up in the corner.*

**Club Promoter**    Young and pretty, we got'em all. She's thirteen. Today is her first day. I have her picture . . . Come and take a look, sir.

**Man One** (*throws up*)    Good things happen on a good day. Bad things happen on a bad day. Then why do I have only bad days? I haven't had a good day since I was born. My birthday was a bad day.

**Man Two**    If it's all out, let's hit the road. If you can't handle the stress from your boss already, how are you gonna work with him?

**Man One**    The drainage system here must be terrible. It stinks everywhere.

**Man Two**    Are you alright? Don't let your boss know you threw up. If he finds out, you're a goner. He'll force you to drink more out of spite.

**Man One**    I can do this. This is nothing.

**Man Two**    Yeah you can.

**Man One**    *Whaaah!* (*Throws up more.*)

**Club Promoter**    What a shitty way to start the day. Are they trying to wreck my business? . . . Come on over. Young and pretty, we got'em all, sir . . . Fucking hell.

**Ji-Hwan** *enters.*

**Club Promoter**    Are you looking to have some fun tonight? Sir, I know a good place. Come with me.

**Ji-Hwan**    Have you ever heard of Park Sung-Tae?

**Club Promoter**    No, I haven't.

**Ji-Hwan**    Something's wrong with you. He used to *own* this town.

**Club Promoter**    You got the wrong guy. This is my first day in this town.

**Ji-Hwan** (*giving him some money*)    I'm not gonna hurt him or anything. I just heard he's here somewhere.

**Club Promoter** *points at the bar behind him with his chin.*

**Ji-Hwan**    He's in there?

**Club Promoter** (*ignores him and continues his job*)    Young and pretty, we got'em all. Come on over. This is a singles' paradise. Come enjoy the hot and gorgeous.

**Ji-Hwan** *enters the bar.*

*Music is blasting, and people are dancing.*

*The music fades during conversations, and in those moments the dances become slower and more erotic.*

*Upstage, there is a bathroom at the top of a low staircase.*

**Bartender**
Today's Special Cocktails!

Bourbon Coke Godfather.
Margarita Kamikaze.
Cocktail Cocktail Special Cocktail.
You need a kiss,
Get the Kiss of Fire.
You want sex,
Get Sex on the Beach.
Cocktail Cocktail Special Cocktail.
You dream of the South,
Get Tropical Blend.
For lovers at dawn,
Get Tequila Sunrise.
Cocktail Cocktail Special Cocktail.

**People** (*chanting along with the* **Bartender** *like a chorus*)
The night, the night, the night
Is young, is young, is young.
Drink up, drink up, drink up!
There's no, there's no, there's no
Tomorrow, tomorrow, tomorrow –
The night, the night, the night
Is young, is young, is young.
Shake it, shake it, shake it!

*Cocktail waitresses, with cocktails in hand, dance erotically and move about the dancing crowd, and people drink and put money into their bras.*

**Ji-Hwan** *gets on the dance stage and looks for* **Sung-Tae**.

**Man Three**   Hey, did you just push me?

**Ji-Hwan**   I'm sorry. My mistake.

**Man Three**   Damn right, your mistake. Are you blind? You made me miss a beat, moron. (*Pushes* **Ji-Hwan**, *who bumps into other people.*)

**Woman One**   Watch it, creep. Don't get so close to me.

**Man Four**   What's your problem, jerk? I feel like shit, and I'm gonna kick your ass.

**Woman Two**   How dare you step on my heels?

**Man Five**   What you looking at, loser?

*A horn sounds, and two dancers jump onto the bar.*

*They remove pieces of clothing one by one, according to the* **Bartender**'s *chant.*

**Bartender**   Yo, this is what you've been waiting for. Give it up for our very special *hors d'oeuvres*!

**Guests** *gather around cheering.*

**Bartender**   Pollution free, 100 per cent natural,

No preservatives, all vegetarian,
Inexperienced, purity itself, brand new,
Thirteen years, four months and twenty-seven days.
Don't let her age full you.
'Cause she's fully bloomed.
28–22–30!

If babies are not your type,
Get the babies out of the way.
Wine gets fine with age.
Maturity, sophistication, impeccable manners
Refined through experience.
If you're looking for something completely unique,
Whips, handcuffs, and cocktails are all available.
33–26–34!

*The gathered guests cheer, waving their bills.*

**Bartender**   Special orders:
Drink companion.
Bed companion.

**Men**   Bed companion, bed companion.

**Bartender**   Bed companion. Bed companion it is!
Spice orders:
Spicy, savory,
Stinging, sharp,
Dainty, sweet.

**Men**   Dainty, sharp.

**Bartender**   Here we go. The auction begins!

**Men**   50,000 won, 100,000 won, 150,000 won, 500,000 won.

**Bartender**   Sold, sold for 500,000 won!
Today's items, all sold out!
Pollution free, dainty spice,
Aged wine, sharp spice,
Sold out, sold out, all sold out!

*The girls on the bar jump down softly and join the men on the stage and dance.*

**Ji-Hwan** *looks at them for a while, frowns, walks downstage, and takes out a cigarette.*

**Girl** (*handing him a beer*)   Why are you alone here? You ran out of money?

**Ji-Hwan**   Do you work here?

**Girl**   It's my first time here. I came to hang out after an exam.

**Ji-Hwan**   How old?

**Girl**   Fifteen.

**Ji-Hwan**   This is no place for a student like you. Your parents must be worried.

**Girl**   We, too, need to relieve our stress. Monthly exams, the nagging, the extra tutoring . . . I'm gonna explode if I don't get to shake it up.

**Ji-Hwan**   Still, this is not a place for you.

**Girl** (*getting close to* **Ji-Hwan** *and touching his body*)   You're naïve, mister. I get it. I was gonna go home anyway. This is lame and too expensive. Can I borrow some money? I ran out.

**Ji-Hwan** *takes out a 10,000 won bill from his wallet and hands it to her.*

**Girl**   . . . Is this for me?

**Ji-Hwan**   No need to pay it back. I'm giving it to you so that you don't come back to a place like this.

**Girl** *laughs out loud and puts the money back in* **Ji-Hwan**'s *pocket.*

**Girl**   It was nice meeting you.

*She leaves* **Ji-Hwan** *and approaches a middle-aged man, who grabs her wrist and heads toward the bathroom.*

**Ji-Hwan** (*stopping the* **Middle-Aged Man**)   Hey, where do you think you're taking her? Let her go. What the hell's gotten into you?

**Middle-Aged Man**   Hey? . . . How old are you, young man? Who taught you to address your elder with "Hey"? Fine, I took the girl you were flirting with. Even so, how dare you address me with "Hey," at such a young age? Do you know what's wrong with this country? Young people like you. Coming to a place like this, when you should be working your ass off. Look at the economy, it's breaking down. But they take away my desk and leave you alone . . . Don't you look down on me, you bastard. Do you know why you live in such prosperity, why you can get drunk here? Because of me. Because of my contribution. But now that they sucked me dry, they spit me out. Why promote me, just to fire me next? Don't look at me like that, young man. The lack of respect in this generation is just appalling.

**Girl** (*to* **Ji-Hwan**)   Wait just a bit. I'll be right back. (*To the* **Middle-Aged Man**.) Darling, let's go.

*They go into the bathroom.*

**Ji-Hwan** (*to the* **Bartender**)   Do you see what's happening here? I'll report you for underage prostitution.

**Bartender**   There must be a misunderstanding, sir. We don't practice anything like that.

**Ji-Hwan** (*pointing at the bathroom*)   A fifteen-year-old girl is trapped in there. Fifteen. She's a child. I just saw her get forced in there! Don't you get it? . . . Fine, come here, I'll show you!

**Bartender**    It sounds like you have a death wish today. (*Two men with metal pipes approach* **Ji-Hwan**.) See them? Don't make no trouble and get out. Maybe you want your money back, but that ain't happening. Amateurs may fall for that. But if you mess with a pro, you're gonna get hurt. (*Hands* **Ji-Hwan** *some bills.*) What's good is good, you know. We all gotta live. If you care about your life, don't make any more trouble. These guys, if you provoke them, they will break your bones.

**Ji-Hwan**    Motherfuckers.

*He tosses the bills, dashes to the bathroom, and opens the curtain.*

**Bartender**    What the fuck –

*The* **Middle-Aged Man** *and the* **Girl** *are up against the white-tiled wall of the men's room, and the* **Girl** *screams.*

**Ji-Hwan**    Take your hands off of her! She's fifteen! She's not even an adult. Even in this fucked-up world, you can't do this to a kid. What if it's your daughter doing this kind of thing? Even when money can buy anything, you still can't do this.

**Middle-Aged Man** *hurriedly pulls up his clothes and exits.*

**Ji-Hwan** (*grabbing the* **Girl**'*s wrist*)    Let's get out of this shithole. Where do you live? Where are your parents?

**Girl** (*grabs an empty bottle from the floor and hits* **Ji-Hwan** *on his head*)    The fuck's wrong with this guy? I finally got a catch after duds all day . . . (*To the* **Middle-Aged Man**.) Hey, fucker, you gotta pay! Get the fuck back here!

**Metal Pipe Men** *hit* **Ji-Hwan**, *who is on the floor, with their pipes.*

**Dancing Crowds** (*chanting to the beat of the pipes*)
   The night, the night, the night
   Is young, is young, is young.
   Drink up, drink up, drink up!
   There's no, there's no, there's no
   Tomorrow, tomorrow, tomorrow –
   The night, the night, the night
   Is young, is young, is young.
   Shake it, shake it, shake it!

*Blackout.*


**Scene Eight**

Setting: Dream and Bar.

*Sound of birds' crying urgently and fluttering their wings in the dark.*

*The stage lights go on and off two or three times, just like a malfunctioning florescent light.*

*Once the stage lights up,* **Joo-Hee** *is looking at* **Ji-Hwan**, *who is sprawled against the bathroom wall.*

**Joo-Hee**    What are you doing here?

**Ji-Hwan**    The floor is so cool.

**Joo-Hee**    You're bleeding from your forehead.

**Ji-Hwan**    I want to sleep.

**Joo-Hee**    Where are we?

**Ji-Hwan**    Where? Where we are . . . . . . I'm sleepy.

**Joo-Hee**    Do you hear that? It's music. I want to dance.

**Ji-Hwan**    Oh, yes, I remember . . . People were drinking and dancing.

**Joo-Hee**    Then what are you doing here?

**Ji-Hwan**    . . . I am . . . looking.

**Joo-Hee**    For whom?

**Ji-Hwan**    . . . I'm going to sleep.

**Joo-Hee**    Looking for what? Did you find it?

**Ji-Hwan**    . . . . . .

**Joo-Hee**    This is fun. They are all drinking and dancing and laughing. Where are we?

**Ji-Hwan**    . . . The Kingdom of Sodom.

**Joo-Hee**    I like it here.

**Ji-Hwan**    . . . You're not supposed to be here.

**Joo-Hee**    I'm gonna go down there. I like it here. I want to hang out with them. Drinking, dancing, drinking, dancing. (*She runs off.*)

**Ji-Hwan**    No, stop, Joo-Hee.

*He manages to get up.*

**Joo-Hee** *stops to look at* **Ji-Hwan**, *then climbs up on the bar.*

**Ji-Hwan**    Joo-Hee. You can't go up there. Come down.

*He stumbles after* **Joo-Hee** *down the stairs.*

*The light flickers on and off, following* **Ji-Hwan**'*s stumbling.*

**Bartender** (*played by* **Gyu-Tae**, *wearing a mask*)    Today's special offering!

**Joo-Hee** *dances erotically to the* **Bartender**'*s announcement.*

**Bartender**    Special discount, low price.
Ten-year-old pickled skate.
It's aged and fermented.
Might make you nauseous.

It's tangy and spicy.
It's pungent and acrid.
Drink companion, bed companion.
It's all on the table.
The auction, the auction, the auction.
The auction begins now.

**Men** (*waving bills*)    10,000 won, 50,000 won, 100,000 won, 500,000 won!

**Ji-Hwan**    I, I got this! Nobody else. 100,000 won. 1,000,000 won!

**Men**    10,000,000 won, 20,000,000 won.

**Bartender**    Sold. Sold for 20,000,000 won.
Today's items, all sold out.
Gone, all gone, completely gone.

**Bartender** *takes off his mask. It is* **Gyu-Tae** *wearing a smile.*

**Ji-Hwan**    You dirty bastard. You killed her, and now you're even selling her. You'll pay for this. I'm not gonna forgive you.

**Joo-Hee** *gently comes down from the bar, goes to the stage, and dances. On the stage, people in masks are dancing slowly.* **Ji-Hwan** *stumbles onto the stage and grabs the masked man, who is dancing with* **Joo-Hee**. *He takes the mask off the man. He turns out to be* **Sung-Tae**.

**Sung-Tae**    Ji-Hwan!

**Ji-Hwan**    . . . (*Falls down.*)

*The bar disappears like magic, and it is a dirty street.*

**Sung-Tae** (*helping up* **Ji-Hwan**)    Did you go insane? What's gotten into you, coming all the way here. Hey, Ji-Hwan, wake up. Getting beaten up like that. . . . . . You can't even fight, you moron, and you drag yourself to this rough part of town.

**Ji-Hwan**    Let's go back . . . Our show opens in two weeks.

**Sung-Tae**    We should go to the hospital.

**Ji-Hwan**    Are you in or out? We're not leaving until you answer.

**Sung-Tae**    I told you I'm out. You think you can guilt me into it, bringing your pathetic self here?

**Ji-Hwan**    Don't let your personal feelings ruin our show. I know you are Gyu-Tae's little brother.

**Sung-Tae** (*grabbing* **Ji-Hwan** *by the throat*)    I'm gonna kick your –

**Ji-Hwan** (*grabbing* **Sung-Tae** *by the throat, using all his strength*)    You all made a commitment. To go all the way. Keep your word. If you don't want to act, you can be on the crew. Coward.

**Sung-Tae**   You're pissing me off – (*He's ready to throw a punch, but* **Ji-Hwan** *falls.*) This moron's so beat-up I can't even hit him anymore.

As **Sung-Tae** *is supporting* **Ji-Hwan** *and is about to leave, a* **Man** *comes out from the bar and throws up at* **Sung-Tae***'s feet.*

**Sung-Tae**   Shit! What a fucked-up day!

*Blackout.*


**Scene Nine**

Setting: Rehearsal Room/Day.

**Jung-Ran** *is humming in the dark, when the stage lights rise. Some are making props or costumes, and* **Hee-Soo** *and* **Jae-Ho** *are lying down downstage.* **Sung-Tae** *is reading the newspaper.*

**Jae-Ho** (*either sighing or yawning*)   Aw – – – – – – –

**Mi-Sun** *sighs.*

**Jung-Ran** *is making costumes with the sewing machine, which makes a "ddddrrr" sound.*

*Something gets stuck in there, and the machine stops working.*

*Silence.*

**Hee-Soo**   Why are they waiting for someone who's not coming?

**Mi-Sun**   Nothing hurts more than waiting. It's like I'm being torn apart here. (*She points to her chest.*)

**Hee-Soo**   Are you also waiting for someone?

**Mi-Sun**   Don't remind me, please. Don't even go there.

*A cell phone rings.* **Jung-Ran** *picks up the phone.*

**Jung-Ran**   Honey. You're late. I've been waiting. I said call every hour . . . Hello, Hello?

**Hee-Soo**   Hard times?

**Mi-Sun**   You bet. He's driving me crazy. Actually totally insane. I would wake up in the middle of the night and yell, "Son of a bitch!," or I'd burst into tears while eating ramen. I put ham and mushroom in it, and he just wouldn't touch it.

**Jae-Ho**   You're a saint.

**Mi-Sun**   Sometimes it feels like I'm choking on my own tears. If only he would take a close look at me, if only he would say my name with affection, but he's nowhere around . . . I'm pathetic, right?

**Jae-Ho**    Why are you still waiting for him?

**Mi-Sun**    Because he's not coming.

**Hee-Soo** (*sighs*)    I give up. What is waiting, really?

**Hyun-Woo**    Get your asses up. We gotta rehearse.

**Hee-Soo**    I'm still not getting it.

**Jae-Ho**    Our show, is it still happening?

**Shin-Ae** *enters.*

**Hyun-Woo**    Did you finish the program edits?

**Shin-Ae**    What are you talking about?

**Hyun-Woo**    I thought you were going to the print shop today.

**Shin-Ae**    I completely forgot.

**Hyun-Woo**    The show opens in a week. Are we selling the programs after closing? You should go there now.

**Shin-Ae** (*plopping down*)    I've been running around all day long, and I just can't. Is there any food left?

**Hyun-Woo**    You really should.

**Shin-Ae**    Hey –

**Hyun-Woo**    Rehearsal's not going well, and now you're screwing up. Stop complaining and do your job.

**Shin-Ae**    I can't anymore. I quit.

**Jae-Ho**    Shin-Ae, come on.

**Shin-Ae**    I went to a job fair today. They say four out of five will not get a job. Get it? Even with a four-year scholarship, a job is not a guarantee. Things are not getting better anytime soon. Do you think I care about our show or the print shop?

**Sung-Tae** (*looking up from his newspaper*)    One more thing. The top thirty corporations are not hiring this year. There will be 380,000 unemployed college graduates this year.

**Shin-Ae**    What's the point of making theatre? Rehearsal's been a disaster. If life sucks, shouldn't theatre be at least fun? But what is this? We're constantly arguing and fighting, and the director is a total tyrant . . . I can't stand it, I'm going insane!

**Hee-Soo**    That's what I'm saying. The frustration is driving me nuts. Sung-Tae, you should take this role again. I just can't. I'm not getting it. Help me out here. You are our Godot.

**Sung-Tae**    We're done, man. If management is out, we're all out. Hey, Mi-Sun, let's go to a club. Show's over.

*A cell phone rings.* **Jung-Ran** *picks up the phone.*

**Jung-Ran**    Honey. If we lost each other, you should call back right away. Switch the service to 013. That one works well.

**Hyun-Woo** (*to* **Jung-Ran**)    Hey, you! Get out!

**Jung-Ran**    ......

**Hyun-Woo**    No cell phone in rehearsal. You should know better.

**Jung-Ran**    We are not rehearsing.

**Hyun-Woo**    This is no time to take a call. Can't you read the room?

**Jung-Ran**    I'm sick of this club! Thank you for nothing! (*Takes her bag and heads out.*)

**Mi-Sun** (*stops* **Jung-Ran**)    Jung-Ran! Come on. Everyone, how about I make some delicious ramen? I'll bring some homemade kimchi and throw in scallions and green onions. Don't you remember? Every day, we sang our club song to live and die for the stage. Let's cheer up and do this thing!

**Mi-Sun** *brings back* **Jung-Ran** *and starts singing the club song, as the others join one by one.*

**Hee-Soo** *brings* **Sung-Tae** *to the stage.*

**Hee-Soo**    It's Godot! Godot is here! (*The others stop singing and look at* **Sung-Tae**, *who has a hat on.*) It's Sung-Tae, on the stage. Godot is here!

**All**    Yeah, Sung-Tae, say your lines. Jae-Ho, join him.

*As* **Sung-Tae** *is about to start,* **Ji-Hwan** *enters.*

**Mi-Sun**    Director, Sung-Tae is back.

**Ji-Hwan**    What are you talking about? The role is Hee-Soo's. Sung-Tae, come down.

**Hee-Soo**    No, Sung-Tae is really back.

**Ji-Hwan**    Are you kidding me?

**Sung-Tae**    I never said I was back. Stop bullshitting, you fag! (*Throws down his hat.*)

**Hee-Soo**    Su—, Sung-Tae.

**Ji-Hwan**    Actors, places. Let's pick up where we left off in Act Two.

**Jae-Ho**    Okay, ready.

*He leads* **Hee-Soo** *to their places under the tree.*

**Ji-Hwan**    Jae-Ho. Let's take it from when they're discussing leaving.

**Jae-Ho** *and* **Hee-Soo** *rehearse the scene from* Waiting for Godot. *Near the end of Act Two, the Boy has left, Estragon just woke up and wants to leave, and Vladimir stops* *him because they have to wait for Godot.* **Ji-Hwan** *watches them rehearse and is dissatisfied with* **Hee-Soo***'s energy.*

**Ji-Hwan**    Hold it, Hee-Soo. You're Vladimir, not Estragon. Do it again and show that you *believe* Godot will come.

**Hee-Soo** (*as* **Vladimir**, *stutters*)    "To wa—, wait for Go—"

**Ji-Hwan**    No. Do it with more confidence. Jae-Ho. From your line.

*They resume rehearsing.*

**Hee-Soo** *still stutters.*

**Sung-Tae** *giggles.*

*This makes* **Hee-Soo** *more insecure, and his voice becomes quieter.*

**Ji-Hwan**    You sound like you've been starving! I know you ate today. Sound like it. It's okay to stutter, but do it loudly.

**Hee-Soo**    . . . . . .

**Ji-Hwan**    . . . Let's think for a minute. Why are these two waiting for Godot for so long? They've repeated the same routine for decades, but why do they still believe Godot is coming?

**Hee-Soo**    What is Godot?

**Ji-Hwan**    It depends. It could be the messiah, a lover . . . or a better world.

**Hee-Soo**    I don't understand abstraction. Give me something specific or I'll get lost.

**Ji-Hwan**    What do you most yearn for in this world?

**Hee-Soo**    . . . . . .

**Ji-Hwan**    Make *that* your Godot. Okay, with that resolved, let's try this again.

**Sung-Tae**    Mi-Sun. After rehearsal, let's go someplace wild.

**Jae-Ho** (*as* **Estragon**) *is annoyed, stares at* **Sung-Tae***, and returns to rehearsing with* **Hee-Soo***.*

**Sung-Tae**    Don't ignore me. Are you in? I know a great spot.

**Jae-Ho**    Shut up, man. I can't focus.

**Sung-Tae**    You heard my whisper? I guess I'm all warmed up.

**Ji-Hwan** (*sighs*)    Keep going.

*Rehearsal continues, while* **Sung-Tae** *keeps talking to* **Mi-Sun***.*

*The director and actors are getting frustrated.*

**Sung-Tae** (*pokes* **Mi-Sun** *when she does not respond*)    Hey, you in?

**Mi-Sun**    No.

**Sung-Tae**   Why?

**Mi-Sun** (*softly*)   We have rehearsal early tomorrow.

**Sung-Tae**   For real? You're not an actor. You don't need Sunday rehearsal.

**Ji-Hwan**   . . . . . . Hee-Soo. Relax and try it again.

**Hee-Soo** (*as Vladimir, with very low energy*)   "To wait for Go—"

**Ji-Hwan**   With confidence. Again –

**Hee-Soo** (*as Vladimir*) *shouts out the line.*

**Ji-Hwan**   That's not it.

**Hee-Soo**   . . . . . .

**Ji-Hwan**   Again.

**Hee-Soo** (*as Vladimir*) *shouting again.*

**Ji-Hwan**   Shouting is not the answer!

**Hee-Soo**   All *you* do is shout! How is yo—, your shou—, shouting supposed to he—, help me?

**Ji-Hwan**   What I mean is, put your heart into the waiting. If you don't feel it in your heart, how would the audience feel it?

**Hee-Soo**   How do I do that?

**Ji-Hwan**   I just told you. Make Godot what you most yearn for in this world. Let us see your yearning.

**Hee-Soo**   How do I ye—, yearn when I don't know what Go—, Go—, Godot is? Am I su—, supposed to tr—, trust someone who ne—, never showed up? Would *you* tr—, trust him?

**Ji-Hwan**   You can yearn for him more because of that very reason.

**Hee-Soo**   I don't even know wh—, what I'm supposed to be waiting for. I me—, mean it. I have n—, no idea. What I wa—, want, who I want to fi—, fight, it's like being in a dark tu—, tunnel with no end in sight, so fru—, frustrating!

**Ji-Hwan**   Make *that* your Godot. Escaping this hopeless frustration. How about that? With that in mind, let's take it from the top.

**Hee-Soo**   I ca—, can't. I've ne—, never escaped from such fru—, frustration. It's ho—, ho—, hopeless.

**Sung-Tae** (*giggles*)   His stuttering is off the roof. By the end of the show, he'll be mute.

**Ji-Hwan**   Shut up!

**Hee-Soo**   Su—, Sung-Tae is right. This is not wo—, working. With this stu—, stu—, stuttering . . . Pl—, please recast before it's to—, too late.

**Ji-Hwan**   It is too late.

**Hee-Soo**   Please.

**Ji-Hwan**   Why give up before you even try? Everybody else is doing it, so why can't you. Stop whining and be a man.

**Hee-Soo**   Pl—, pl—, please stop saying that! Some pe—, people can't be a ma—, man, and some pe—, people ca—, can't do it. Wh—, why are you all fo—, forcing me to do things I re—, really can't do!

**Ji-Hwan**   Shut up, we have one more week. Whine less and practice more. On your feet! Jae-Ho, go.

**Jae-Ho** (*as Estragon*)   Okay. "Where shall we—." (To **Hee-Soo**.) . . . Hey, we're going. "Where shall we—."

**Hee-Soo** *tries to say his lines.*

*But he is so stressed out that what comes out is a mix of cries, silences, and outbursts.*

**Jae-Ho** *stops.*

**Jae-Ho**   . . . Shall I continue?

**Ji-Hwan** (*sighs*)   Let's stop here.

**Hee-Soo**   It's not wo—, working. I do—, don't understand this pl—, play. What are we wa—, waiting for, why are we wa—, waiting this ha—, hard for someone who is not co—, coming? I, I, I, I –

*As his words are not coming, he punches himself in frustration.*

Just do—, do—, don't get it.

**Jae-Ho**   Hee-Soo! (*Grabs* **Hee-Soo** *from behind.*) Don't do this. Just don't –

**Ji-Hwan**   . . . To be honest, I don't get it, either. Why these folks wait for Godot who is obviously not coming, what am I waiting for, or am I even waiting?

**Hyun-Woo**   Ji-Hwan.

**Ji-Hwan**   But still, we can't just give up now. We haven't even got to the end. Despair can wait till then. For now, though, let's continue rehearsing. Get it, you moron?

**Hee-Soo**   . . . . . .

**Ji-Hwan**   Jae-Ho, let's clean up. Get the others. (**Jae-Ho** *exits.*) Sung-Tae. How's the lighting plan?

**Sung-Tae** (*opens the newspaper loudly*)   Lights on at the beginning, lights off at the end, right?

**Ji-Hwan**   It's your job, so do it right.

**Sung-Tae**    I never said I'd do it. You threw this on me.

**Ji-Hwan**    Don't be a smartass. You can ruin everything we've worked for.

**Sung-Tae**    That sounds very serious. So if this fails, it's all on me.

**Ji-Hwan**    Bring the lighting plan by tomorrow.

**Sung-Tae**    And a stuttering actor and an incompetent director guarantee a hit.

**Ji-Hwan**    Sung-Tae, don't.

**Sung-Tae** (*puts the paper down and gets up*)    Okay. I'll do it. Hey, Mi-Sun, let's hit the club.

**Mi-Sun**    Jerk.

**Sung-Tae**    What's the matter with you? Did I say something wrong? This production was rotten from the start. How are we supposed to put up a show with a stuttering actor? All the director does is yell.

**Hee-Soo** *rushes out.*

**Ji-Hwan**    Hee-Soo!

**Hyun-Woo** (*from offstage*)    Hey Hee-Soo, where you going?

**Sung-Tae**    This show is not happening. Let's stop wasting our time and hit the club.

**Ji-Hwan** *hits* **Sung-Tae** *with the script.*

**Sung-Tae**    So this is the moment your patience runs out! Is that all you got?

**Ji-Hwan**    You are a bitter loser, just like your brother. (*Throws down the script.*)

**Sung-Tae**    What did you just say? You shithead, say that again!

**Ji-Hwan**    I said you are just like your crazy brother. You don't give a shit about what others are feeling, how others are hurting. You will do anything to get what you want.

**Sung-Tae**    Don't you dare bring up my brother. You don't deserve to utter his name, when you haven't lost anything!

**Ji-Hwan** *loses it completely as his accumulated stress finally explodes. He picks up a stick and beats* **Sung-Tae** *mercilessly.* **Sung-Tae** *takes it without any resistance.*

**Ji-Hwan** (*confused, momentarily identifies* **Sung-Tae** *as* **Gyu-Tae** *during his outburst*)    She's dead, you bastard. She just turned twenty. Joo-Hee would be alive if it wasn't for Gyu-Tae. How could you let her just run to her death? And now your cruelty is killing somebody else! Did her death mean anything at all? The world isn't any better, but she's dead, and you're alive. Why!

**Mi-Sun** *screams, as* **Jae-Ho** *and* **Hyun-Woo** *run in and stop* **Ji-Hwan**.

**Hyun-Woo**    Ji-Hwan, are you crazy? You're gonna kill him.

**Sung-Tae**    How come *you're* alive? Why aren't you dead? No, you don't get to speak like that. You couldn't even go crazy. You alone survived, without as much as a scratch! Don't stop him. Bring it on, man. Is that all you got!

*Sound of pepper fog spray like a hallucination.* **Ji-Hwan**, *in a manic state, starts hitting* **Jae-Ho** *and* **Hyun-Woo**. **Mi-Sun** *jumps on* **Ji-Hwan***'s back but falls off, and she tries again and again.*

*In the background, in silhouette or a faint projection, military police are beating student protesters, while* **Joo-Hee***'s loud reading of the protest address is heard. The tension grows.*

**Ji-Hwan** *and* **Mi-Sun** *talk over one another.*

**Ji-Hwan**    Yes, I'm alive. My friend died, and I didn't. She was in flames, dying right in front of me . . . But I couldn't do anything. I just watched . . . . . . I killed her . . . I really did! . . . I was too scared to save her . . . Flames were all over her . . . But I couldn't do anything! . . . Die! . . . Trash like you have no place here . . . Fuck this world!

**Mi-Sun** (*desperately piggybacking on* **Ji-Hwan**)    Sung-Tae, get out! . . . Ji-Hwan! What's wrong with you? You know Sung-Tae doesn't mean what he says. He's hurting, too . . . It's not just you. We all are . . . Sung-Tae is devastated . . . Get out, Sung-Tae. If you don't get out now . . . There's no stopping him.

**Ji-Hwan** *inadvertently hits* **Mi-Sun**. **Mi-Sun***'s scream overlaps with* **Joo-Hee***'s scream, as the background turns red.* **Ji-Hwan** *stands still.*

*Silence. A long silence.*

**Mi-Sun**    Remember what you said to Hee-Soo. We didn't even get to the end. Despair . . . could wait till then. We can't give up now.

**Ji-Hwan**    . . . . . .

*Blackout.*


**Scene Ten**

Setting: Rehearsal Room/Night.

*The light flickers.*

*In the dark, the door creaks open, and* **Ji-Hwan** *enters. He is holding a soju bottle.*

**Ji-Hwan**    It's o—, over. All over. This musty smell, this show. Done.

**Joo-Hee** (*offstage*)    Hey, Ji-Hwan.

**Ji-Hwan**    Hi, Joo-Hee. It's me. I'm here.

**Joo-Hee** (*offstage*)    Are you done with the show?

**Ji-Hwan**   Yes, I'm done. I'm out.

**Sung-Tae** (*only his voice in the dark*)   Who's there . . . Damn, what's wrong with this light? Where's the power switch?

*The light comes on.* **Jae-Ho** *and others are all sleeping on the floor, and* **Sung-Tae** *is sitting in front of the lighting board.* **Jae-Ho** *snores from time to time.*

**Ji-Hwan**   Did you spend the night here?

**Sung-Tae**   This is just great. We open in a few days, and the director is drunk.

**Ji-Hwan**   You worked on the lighting all night long?

**Sung-Tae**   There's no show without the lighting.

**Ji-Hwan** (*laughs*)   Are you alright?

**Sung-Tae**   I'm fine. I'll do the lighting even with a broken arm. (*He lifts his hand, which is wrapped up in gauze.*) I do what I gotta do. (*He moves the dimmer. The light flickers.*)

**Jae-Ho** (*in his sleep*)   Hee-Soo, from the top . . . From the top.

**Ji-Hwan**   You're doing it all wrong. You have to be patient. Your hand has to be in sync with your mind.

**Sung-Tae**   Tell me about it. But my hand is not working.

**Ji-Hwan** (*holds* **Sung-Tae**'*s hand from behind and helps him move the dimmer*)   See. It works . . . like this. In sync. Equipment is just like a human being. If you push it too hard, it will eventually break. You have to be patient with it and wait for it to open up to you. Move the dimmer gently and breathe with it –

**Sung-Tae**   If you don't trust me, find somebody else. (*He picks up his bag and gets up.*) I stayed up all night working, and you got wasted.

**Ji-Hwan**   Don't go, Sung-Tae . . . I thought, even until just a few minutes ago, this was all over. Done. The end . . . But you know what? When I opened the door here, the world was still going. The light flickered and then it came on . . . We haven't tried everything yet, the audience is waiting, and it's not over yet.

**Sung-Tae** (*throwing down his bag*)   Stop being melodramatic. (*Pushes* **Ji-Hwan** *aside and sits at the lighting board.*) Out of my way, . . . So move the dimmer gently, and then what? . . . You stink, man. How much did you drink? (*Responding to* **Ji-Hwan**'*s touch.*) Ow, be gentle with me.

**Hee-Soo** *enters, drying his wet face with a towel.*

**Hee-Soo** (*bows to* **Ji-Hwan**)   Good morning. Wake up, Jae-Ho. We have to rehearse.

**Jae-Ho** (*in his sleep*)   Hee-Soo. Don't try so hard . . . Just be yourself, man . . . I'll have spicy seafood noodle.

**Ji-Hwan**    Let him sleep. I'll fill in for him.

**Hee-Soo**    No, that's okay. Jae-Ho, please wake up.

**Ji-Hwan**    . . . Come on. Be my sparring partner.

**Sung-Tae**    Ji-Hwan's wasted. Completely.

**Ji-Hwan**    You rehearsed all night long. Do it like your life depends on it.

**Hee-Soo**    Ji-Hwan.

**Ji-Hwan**    What now?

**Hee-Soo**    I, have my Godot. But what if it never comes?

**Ji-Hwan** (*laughs*)    What is it?

**Hee-Soo** (*stutters once in a while*)    Not running away from this show. Finishing this damn show, even if I stutter, even if the audience laughs at me. Not being intimidated when people call me pe—, pervert. . . . Not saying so—, sorry to my dad, even when he beats me with a golf club. I don't wa—, want what he wants. I hate being the eldest, I hate being a son . . . . . . I hate being a ma—, man. I'm just me.

*Sound of birds clattering.*

**Ji-Hwan**    Can you hear that, Hee-Soo? Birds are clattering on the roof.

**Joo-Hee**    Ji-Hwan's favorite sound, birds clattering.

**Ji-Hwan**    I always liked this sound. The sound of birds clattering brought me warmth, lit up the dark rehearsal room, eliminated my aches, frustrations, and worries, and even made me want to hug Gyu-Tae who always drove me crazy. If only he could hear that clattering sound in the morning . . . I feel like I can do this, really do this.

**Hee-Soo** (*to* **Ji-Hwan**)    Can I, really be your sparring partner? . . . If we keep waiting, will Go—, Godot finally come?

**Jae-Ho**    Hee-Soo, from the top . . . Let's do this, you bastard.

**Hee-Soo** (*hands* **Ji-Hwan** *the shoes that were next to* **Jae-Ho**)    Let's do this.

**Ji-Hwan** (*as Estragon*)    Hey, Sung-Tae. Cue the lights.

**Sung-Tae**    . . . Yes, sir. Cueing the lights.

*The lights come on.*

**Ji-Hwan** *and* **Hee-Soo** *look at each other for a moment.*

*There is the sound of birds' wings fluttering.*

*End of Play.*

## Notes

1    Brecht, Bertolt. 1949. "A Short Organum for the Theatre." *Brecht on Theatre: The Development of an Aesthetic.* Ed. and trans. John Willett. London: Methuen, 1964. pp. 196.

2    Hangover soup is used to cure hangovers the morning after a night of drinking. It is called *haejang-guk* or *sulguk* and usually contains meat and vegetables boiled in bone broth.

3    *Oppa* literally means a girl's older brother. The term is used when a girl or a woman addresses her older brother, or a slightly older boy, or a man. It is also a term of affection used between close friends or in romantic relationships.

4    OB: "Old Boy." OB refers to the cohort from the previous generation, that of Ji-Hwan and Seung-Jae.

5    The April Revolution, also called the April 19 Revolution, occurred in 1960 as mass protests against President Syngman Rhee.

6    The Gwangju Uprising was an armed uprising of local citizens of the city of Gwangju against soldiers and government police, which lasted from May 18 to May 27, 1980. It is also called: "*O-il-pahl*" ("오일팔," Five-One-Eight in Korean), the Gwangju Democratization Struggle, the Gwangju Massacre, or the May 18 Democratic Uprising.

7    Myeongdong Cathedral is the national cathedral of the Roman Catholic Archdiocese of Seoul, and its official full name is the Cathedral Church of the Virgin Mary of the Immaculate Conception. It is located in Myeongdong in Junggu, Seoul, and is a highly populated commercial area, filled with various department stores and shops, restaurants, and tourist attractions.

8    Translated by Walter Byongsok Chon from Myung-Wha Kim's Korean text, with reference to Büchner's original *Dantons Tod* (1835). Original German Text: "Ich frage nun [. . .] Wir werden unserm Satze noch einige Schlüsse hinzuzufügen haben; sollen einige hundert Leichen uns verhindern, sie zu machen? Moses führte sein Volk durch das Rote Meer und in die Wüste, bis die alte verdorbne Generation sich aufgerieben hatte, eh' er den neuen Staat gründete. Gesetzgeber! Wir haben weder das Rote Meer noch die Wüste, aber wir haben den Krieg und die Guillotine. Die Revolution ist wie die Töchter des Pelias: sie zerstückt die Menschheit, um sie zu verjüngen. Die Menschheit wird aus dem Blutkessel wie die Erde aus den Wellen der Sündflut mit urkräftigen Gliedern sich erheben, als wäre sie zum ersten Male geschaffen."

9    A Korean underground rock group that was formed in 1994 and made their official debut in 1997. The band released four albums and is known for their experimental sound, parodying other genres and using minimal musical instrumentation, as well as its nonsensical lyrics and performances that would fall in the range of performance art. The major networks banned their songs for their pessimism and hopelessness. The band did the soundtrack for the major hit 2002 movie *Sympathy for Mr. Vengeance*, directed by Chan-Wook Park. The band has a strong cult following, and their albums are now rare items sold at high prices at underground markets.

# Oedipus: The Fate of the Story

## 오이디푸스: 이야기의 운명

A full-length drama

By Myung-Wha Kim
Translated from Korean into English by Walter Byongsok Chon
English Language Translation Consultant: Anne M. Hamilton

© 2026 by Byongsok Chon
All rights reserved

* The Korean production of *Oedipus: The Fate of the Story* premiered at ARKO Arts Theater the Korean Culture and Arts Center as part of the 2000 Seoul Theater Festival, under the direction of Gwangbo Kim.

* This play has been translated with official permission from the author. The contract is available upon inquiry.

* The Daesan Foundation awarded a 2022 Grant for the Translation of Korean Literary Works to Walter Byongsok Chon and Anne Hamilton to create *An English Theatrical Translation of Korean Plays by Myung-Wha Kim*. This collection of four plays includes several genres exploring Korean history, culture, and sentiments, thereby enhancing intercultural theatrical exchange. Walter Byongsok Chon is the translator and Anne Hamilton is the English language translation consultant. The collection includes *Birds Don't Use a Crosswalk*, *Oedipus: The Fate of the Story*, *Sound of the Moon*, and *The Wind's Desire*.

* The translator and English language translation consultant were each awarded a Fellowship by the Bogliasco Foundation, and completed Spring 2024 Residencies in Bogliasco, Italy. *An English Theatrical Translation of Korean Plays by Myung-Wha Kim* was created with the support of a Bogliasco Foundation Fellowship.

Walter Byongsok Chon

© 2026 by Byongsok Chon
All rights reserved

## Characters

**Old Poet**
**Oedipus**
**Sphinx**
**Boy**
**Senior Ministers (Senior Minister One, Senior Minister Two, Senior Minister**
**Three, Senior Minister Four)**
**Creon**
**Petitioners**
**Young People (Young Person One, Young Person Two, Young Person Three,**
**Young Person Four)**
**Young Poet**
**Jocasta**
**High Priest**
**Tiresias**
**Macbeth**
**Citizens of Thebes (Citizen One, Citizen Two, Citizen Three)**
**Guard**
**Old Man (Witness) One**
**Old Man (Witness) Two**
**Antigone**

## Time and Place

Ancient Greece
Thebes, The Temple of Hades, Colonus Forest

## Scenes

**Notes on the Text**

\* The translation follows the original text's punctuation as much as possible in order to reflect the original language's pacing and the author's intention. The ellipses ". . . . . .", ". . .", and "–" appear in the Korean text.

> Note: In Western script notation, the playwright's use of ". . . . . ." can be interpreted as being similar to a (*Pause.*).
> Accordingly, ". . ." is similar to a (*Beat.*).
> And "–" is similar to a breath.

\* Notes provide explanations of specific Korean references for the reader's convenience.
\* This play contains lyrical lines recited by the Old Poet and the Boy. The playwright has intended for these recitations to be delivered poetically. However, she has stated that she is also open to the possibility of them being performed as songs, with new music composed.

**Content Warning**

*This play contains physical violence.*

## Scene One: Prologue

Setting: Lobby of the Theatre, Before the Curtain.

*White-haired* **Old Poet** *wanders around the lobby, playing the flute.*


## Scene Two: Once Upon a Time

*Flute music heard in the darkness.*

**Old Poet**  A story for sale . . . An ancient story, with a true lesson. About a man who was brave but rash, who was honorable but suffered. About how insolence and greed led to ruin. Some food and shelter for the night, that's all I ask.

*The* **Old Poet** *sits in a corner.*

**Old Poet**  Lord, it's a night out in the dew for me. (*Plays a sad tune with the flute for a bit.*) Have you heard? What happened to the Cadmus household, who ruled Thebes? Let me tell you about Cadmus' descendant Laius, and his son Oedipus. (*Plays the flute.*)

*A desolate land with rocks of peculiar shapes.*

**Oedipus** *enters, in good health, with a cane and in traveling attire.*

**Old Poet** (*recites to* **Oedipus**, *who is not aware of him*)
My friend, you are trembling.
The night is frightening and pitch-black.
You can open your eyes.
But you cannot see ahead.
So life is frightening, indeed.
Still keep your eyes open.
When only nightmares await you
In the dark, it's time to hear
The story of Oedipus.

**Oedipus** (*to himself*)  Over this mountain lies Thebes. Go a little bit farther, and maybe I'll sleep like a man tonight. But first, let's stop for a moment. Eyes can be deceiving. My destination, as close as it may seem, can in fact be miles ahead. An empty stomach makes you see things.

**Sphinx** *heavy breathing.*

**Oedipus**  Do stones breathe in Thebes? Show yourself at once.

**Sphinx** *shows itself slowly in the background.*

**Oedipus**  Who could even be in this desolate rocky land, with no vegetation, under the scorching sun? I haven't seen a soul in over a month. Even a thief, I would love to see. I am Oedipus, the lonely being.

**Sphinx**  Who dares to set foot in my territory?

**Oedipus**    . . . A woman's torso, a lion's legs, and an eagle's wings? You are the famous monster guarding the gate of Thebes.

**Sphinx**    I'm not a monster, I am the Sphinx. If you want to enter, you must solve my riddle. Look at all these skeletons on the ground. This is what happens if you don't solve the riddle. Run for your life if this frightens you.

**Oedipus**    You're telling me I have to go down this rocky road and cross that eerie lake again? I miss people, Sphinx. I'd die for a warm meal or a warm woman.

**Sphinx**    You will beg me to spare your life.

**Oedipus**    Nope, you're wrong about that. I am Oedipus, and I don't fear death.

**Sphinx**    Immature! I thought you were a brave one, but you're a child with no understanding of fate. Life, as long as it may seem to you, young man, is but a dream. In the blink of an eye, you're rotting in the ground. That's fate. In the face of fate, power and glory are but illusions, and honor and love are but vanities. And you say you don't fear death? Fine, then solve this riddle.

**Old Poet**    "What walks on four legs in the morning, two legs in the afternoon, and three legs in the evening?" The Sphinx asked the riddle, and Oedipus solved it. It's Human.

**Sphinx**    What plans ahead but never knows what's around the corner?

**Oedipus**    . . . Human. I planned ahead to come to Thebes but didn't see you around the corner.

**Sphinx**    What eats its own flesh?

**Oedipus**    Eats its own flesh?

**Sphinx**    Insolent one, prepare to die.

**Oedipus** (*drawing his sword*)    That's for me to say. The answer is obviously Human. Do you know why I left my hometown and travelled all the way here, Sphinx? Because of my heartless father, who spent his youth in the battlefield, and who, in his old age, almost killed me based on a foolish priest's prophesy that I would take his throne. So what eats its own flesh and blood and kills its own, blinded by power? The answer is Human.

**Sphinx**    Impressive. Since you solved the riddle, I will give you a reward: the power everyone desires, the ability to see the future and perceive human nature. The elixir of life, so that you can defy fate and live forever. You will no longer fear. You will no longer look behind your back for the assassins hiding in the dark.

**Oedipus** (*puts down his sword hesitatingly*)    So, you're really going to give me all of that?

**Sphinx**    Come close. Mere being, who is brave but not immortal, and bright but not prescient. I challenge you, human, to resist this sweet temptation. Your fate lies there, finite being.

**Oedipus** Temptation, sweet as honey and colorful as oleander. Do I trust that? I am hesitant, reluctant, and uncertain. Words can be cunning. Your words are choking me, like ropes from the gallows. But what was my oath, as I ran away after beheading the priest who upset my father? . . . Never trust an Oracle. So listen to me, Sphinx. If it is fate that I succumb to your temptation, I choose to challenge that fate. Instead of the elixir of life, I choose the death of you and peace on Thebes. (*Lifts his sword and strikes the* **Sphinx** *down*)

*Gong sound.*

*Complete silence as everything disappears.*

*Spotlight on the* **Old Poet** *in the corner.*

## Scene Three: The Song of the Old Poet

**Old Poet** (*recites*)
>  Oedipus, King of Kings –
>  Bearer of peace, honor of Thebes
>  Solves the riddle of death.
>  Thebes opens its gates
>  And welcomes its new King.
>  Oedipus, *Hurrah*!
>  King of Kings.

**Boy** *from Colonus looks at the* **Old Poet**.

**Boy** Who are you, old man?

**Old Poet** Who's speaking?

**Boy** This is King Theseus' land. Strangers are not welcome.

**Old Poet** Young master, I am merely passing by. I'm not hurting anyone. The world needs more compassion, the harder people's lives become. I beg you for a meal and a bed for the night. (**Boy** *throws a stone.*) What a harsh world. I can see people are suffering from war and famine, but this is no way to treat a guest. God will punish you for this. What town would tolerate such rudeness?

**Boy** (*laughs*) This is Colonus. High debts and the war are causing great damage. But the people of Colonus know how to protect themselves. We refuse interaction with sub-human beings.

**Old Poet** Did you say Colonus? Colonus of Athens?

**Boy** It is so. The sacred forest protects us.

**Old Poet** (*on his knees*) Thank you, young master. If this is indeed Colonus, I'll be happy without a roof and be covered in dew. I've finally reached my destination, after a long, long trip. If you let me stay a night, I will reward you with the story of Oedipus the King.

**Boy**    Oedipus, that lunatic who killed his own father? . . . Who the hell are you?

**Old Poet**    A mere storyteller passing by. (*Plays the flute.*)

**Boy**    That's a beautiful sound. So what happened with this Oedipus guy? Tell me about him. (*Sits by the* **Old Poet**.)

*Blackout.*


## Scene Four: The Wrath of the Gods

Setting: In Front of the Gates of Thebes.

*Ominous drum sound.*

*Smell of incense. As the stage lights up, a group of* **Petitioners** *are burning incense and praying.*

*From one side of the stage,* **Creon** *and* **Senior Ministers** *are looking at the* **Petitioners***.*

**Senior Minister One**    Three years of drought.

**Senior Minister Two**    Zeus used to endow us with rain in the winter, but he must have left Thebes. Maybe he's somewhere in Egypt or Crete having an affair.

**Senior Minister Three**    The forecaster says the wind smells different. That it's about time Euros brings us some rain.

**Senior Minister Four**    He said the same thing ten days ago.

**Senior Minister One**    And a month ago. He predicted torrential rain, based on the irregular movement of the moon.

**Senior Minister Two**    Creon. What do we do?

**Creon**    . . .

**Senior Minister Three**    Listen to the drums. I'm afraid people will revolt.

**Senior Minister Four**    A gathering like that spreads the epidemic even further.

**Senior Minister One**    The King is out, doing construction with that crazy crew.

**Senior Minister Two**    We must do something about this. Even the weather is telling us.

**Creon**    By Zeus! Here comes Oedipus the King.

**Oedipus** *and his young construction crew run in energetically.*

**Creon** *and the* **Senior Ministers** *welcome him.*

**Senior Ministers**    Your Majesty, we salute you. (*They perform the salute dance.*)

**Oedipus**    Stop that. The three-year-long extreme heat can kill a strong young person, and you're doing that long dance with your brittle bodies? You'll get heatstroke. No more ceremonies during a drought.

**Senior Minister One**   Impossible.

**Senior Minister Two**   Your Majesty. To ban the dance, you have to follow the procedure.

**Oedipus**   Then follow the procedure.

**Senior Minister Three**   This dance symbolizes the authority of the royal family and the Senior Ministry.

**Creon**   Follow the King's order. The King prioritizes practicality and progress over authority and tradition.

**Senior Ministers**   Creon!

**Creon**   Moreover, that dance is so long that it makes the citizens uncomfortable. Even you complained about it, when you missed a beat or two after getting drunk the night before. The King is doing you a favor. Laws that are behind the times must be changed.

**Oedipus**   That's my Creon. These grandpas would have killed me with their stubbornness already, if it weren't for you, dear brother-in-law.

**Senior Ministers**   Your dignity is overwhelming.

*They perform the dance of apology.*

**Oedipus**   Ban the dance of apology as well. Thebes is burning up, you're perspiring from the dance, and now I'm fuming from the heat. (*Looks at the* **Petitioners**.) Who are they? That's a sight I didn't see last month.

**Creon**   They are petitioners, praying for rain.

**Oedipus**   I banned praying for rain last year.

**Creon**   The three-year-long drought is causing extreme fear in the people.

**Oedipus**   And prayers will solve that? Then why did we fail last year and the year before? It's a drain on national treasury. Ban it at once.

**Creon**   The people have reached their breaking point.

**Senior Minister Three**   Infectious diseases are killing livestock and making people sick.

**Senior Minister Four**   Banning prayers for rain might lead to revolt.

**Oedipus** (*to the* **Senior Ministers**)   The cause of all this lies in your cowardice.

**Senior Ministers**   Your dignity is overwhelming. (*They perform the dance of apology again.*)

**Creon**   By Zeus! His Majesty just banned that dance.

**Senior Ministers**   *Ohthatsrightthatsrightthatsrightthatsrightthatsright*!

**Oedipus**   Just get through this year.

**Creon**   Then what, Your Majesty?

**Oedipus**   Dear brother-in-law. The construction is in its final stage. In a few months, we can bring the water from the lake into the castle. We could have done it much sooner, if we had invested more in construction and less in praying for rain over the dry wells.

**Creon**   That is good news, Your Majesty.

**Senior Minister Three**   Since construction is almost done, we ask Your Majesty to consider removing yourself from such menial labor. It is not fitting for Your Majesty to lift rocks and dig in the ground like a slave.

**Oedipus**   Look at these arms. The menial labor made my arms as strong as an ox. I can even beat Hercules.

**Senior Minister One**   Think of the crown shining on your head, Your Majesty. Lifting rocks and digging do not befit the crown.

**Oedipus**   Do not befit the crown?

*He throws the crown in the air, and his crew catches it in excitement.*

**Senior Ministers** (*short scream*)

**Senior Minister Two**   The crown is sacred, Your Majesty. How could you toss the crown that graced the heads and hands of previous kings!

**Senior Minister Three**   And with one hand!

**Senior Minister Four**   The crown is the symbol of the King.

**Oedipus**   No, it isn't. I am the King, King Oedipus. The only King in this state. A lion without its mane would still be fierce and menacing. Even without my crown, I am still Oedipus, the King of Thebes.

**Young Person One**   Your Majesty, does the crown make a King? (*Putting the crown on his head.*) Then I am the King.

*The young crew members take turns wearing the crown.*

**Young Person Two** (*with a crown on, imitating a pot belly*)   I am the previous King Laius.

**Young Person Three** (*limping*)   Then I am Cadmus, the founder of Thebes.

**Senior Minister One**   How incredibly rude. Return the crown to His Majesty.

**Senior Ministers**   The crown symbolizes the King's authority.

**Young Poet** (*puts on the crown but gets intimidated by the* **Senior Ministers** *and is about to give it back to* **Oedipus**)   Your Majesty, please take the crown.

**Young Person Two** (*takes the crown, puts it on, and imitates a hunchback*)   What kind of a King am I, little ones? Show your respect to the crown. The crown symbolizes the King's authority. (*The* **Young People** *mock the* **Senior Ministers**' *salute dance. They giggle.*)

**Senior Minister Four**    Outrageous. Impudent rascals. Your Majesty, these are traitors and conspirators. Punish them at once. How dare they disrespect the King, while riding on his coattails.

**Senior Ministers**    Tear apart their limbs and kill all their relatives!

**Oedipus**    Calm down, Senior Ministers. Killing them when the construction is not completely finished means it will never be completed. When everybody else called me insane for this construction plan, these young people stepped in and devoted their lives to building the waterway. Now, you adrenaline-thirsty bandits—give me back my crown. Swear on your life that you will not touch this crown again as long as I'm alive.

**Young People**    We swear, Your Majesty.

*They give him back the crown.*

**Senior Minister Three**    With both hands! Please use both hands, Your Majesty.

**Oedipus**    Okay, I'll use both hands. Now that I have my crown back, let's get to the point. How can we comfort the people, without wasting our national treasury on prayers for rain? What did we do in the past?

**Senior Minister One**    We can consult the Oracle.

**Senior Minister Two**    Paying the Oracle is more economical than praying for rain. It only costs one pouch of spice and five gold coins.

**Oedipus**    I hate the Oracle.

**Senior Minister Three**    Delphi is not far from here.

**Oedipus**    . . . . . . Once upon a time a crook priest prophesied that I would kill my father and marry my mother. That damn oracle cost me my royal inheritance and sent me into exile. If it wasn't for my mother's desperate plea for my life, my father would have killed me then and there.

**Young Poet**    Your Majesty, that heinous Oracle's prophecy widely spread all across Greece. The previous King Laius had his own son killed, based on that oracle.

**Petitioners** *hit the drum—the sound of a boom.*

*Silence.*

*A baby's cry, like an echo.*

**Creon** (*aside*)    That's right! . . . That's what happened. I had blocked it from my memory for a long time, but I can see it like it was yesterday,

**Oedipus**    Do you know how mortifying it is, to be banished by your own father and to wander around foreign lands? I was so hot-blooded I fought everything that got in my way. Once I fought a group of thieves at a three-way intersection. Even when I encountered that creature, the Sphinx, I was more intrigued than afraid.

**Creon**    Your Majesty, let's consult the Oracle.

**Oedipus**    I said no Oracle!

**Creon**    If the prayers are not working, the people might consider human sacrifice. We already offer ten humans to the Minotaur of Crete each year.

**Oedipus**    Shit. (*Drums—the sounds of boom boom boom*)    Alright, let's consult the Oracle. What chance can there really be that this Oracle will dictate that I kill my own offspring? Creon, let's get ready. We're leaving for Delphi at dawn tomorrow.

**Creon**    No! You've been away for over a month building the dam. If you leave again, the public unrest will grow further.

**Senior Minister One**    But we are desperate.

**Senior Minister Two** (*cutting off* **Senior Minister One**)    Let's listen to Creon.

**Creon**    I'll go myself. The previous King always appointed me for consultations with the Oracle.

**Senior Minister Three**    Let's listen to Creon.

**Oedipus**    I approve. I trust you, dear brother-in-law.

**Creon**    It is my honor, Your Majesty. In the meantime, please take extra care of your royal mind and body. Just in time, here comes your shelter, my sister.

**Oedipus**    Oh my, she's as skinny as a stick.

**Creon**    She's been fasting, praying for your safe return.

**Jocasta**    My King, you have returned! When my mirror broke all of a sudden, I got so afraid something might have happened to you.

**Oedipus**    Something happened to *you*, My Queen. In only a month, you grew pale as the moon. (*To* **Creon**.) It should be you going to Delphi, dear brother-in-law. If I leave again, she'll be eclipsed.

**Jocasta**    Hello, everyone, I want to hear all about your construction adventures. When will you finish? I bet it was my dear King Oedipus who was the strongest and bravest of you all under the scorching sun and at that eerie lake.

**Young Person One**    His Majesty was the only one who could lift heavy stones with the lever.

**Young Poet**    He named the waterway Jocasta after you, My Queen.

**Oedipus**    That's enough. Stop your chattering and leave us alone.

**Young Person Two**    A stone crushed a worker, and His Majesty –

**Oedipus**    Asinine cows. Do you really think she wants to listen to you? One more word, and you will feel my wrath. Go to the tavern and get some rest. Get out of my sight and get wasted for two nights and three days. This is an order. Creon, they're all yours. (*To the* **Young Poet**.) Play a tune for Jocasta.

**Oedipus** *and* **Jocasta** *exit.*

**Creon**    Good work, everyone. Soon Thebes will no longer suffer from the drought. I'm proud of you all. You are the future of Thebes. You deserve better than getting wasted at a shabby tavern. Buy some fancy clothes and enjoy yourselves at a dignified bordello. Here is some gold. (*Gives them gold coins.*)

**Young People** (*cheering*)    Oedipus –
Oedipus –
Oedipus –
Someday
A new era will dawn.

**Young Person One**    Down with the olden days.

**Young Person Two**    Mute the senile elders.

**Young Person Three**    Raise the flag of reform.

**Young Person One**    A new era, a new world.

**Young Person Two**    We are the new leaders.

**Young Person Three**    The new world belongs to us.

**Young People**    With Oedipus –

**Young Poet** *plays the flute.*

**Senior Ministers**
Oedipus –
Oedipus –
Oedipus –

**Young People** (*recite*)
He solved the riddle of the Sphinx,
Opened the gates of Old Thebes,
And added a big rock
To the old one on its shoulders.
Ladies of the bordello
Smile upon the new world.
Fuck the old authority.
The new world belongs to us.

*The* **Young People** *swear at the* **Senior Ministers** *and exit, except for the* **Young Poet**.

**Senior Ministers** (*recite*)
Someday,
We knew a new era would dawn.
Horrendous era, horrendous world.
They are the new hegemony.
The new world bows to them.
Fools are rushing in,

Weighing down elders' wings.
We'll teach them a good lesson.
Creon,
Why so quiet?

**Creon**    I like them. They are skilled, ambitious, and loyal. Even with gold, they keep chanting Oedipus.

Oedipus –.

Oedipus –.

Oedipus –.

**Senior Minister One** (*to the other* **Senior Ministers**)    How insolent.

**Senior Minister Two**    Worst of the worst.

**Senior Minister Three**    Horny pervert.

**Senior Minister Four**    His wife could be his mother.

**Senior Minister One**    Instead of worshipping the Gods.

**Senior Minister Two**    He wastes the national treasury on construction.

**Senior Minister Three**    And confiscates the inherited wealth from the Senior Ministry.

**Senior Minister Four**    And expects the people's approval?

As a newcomer in an old land?

**Senior Ministers**    Huh – ! No way.

Over our dead bodies.

We are not backing down.

**Senior Minister One**    Impudent puppets of Oedipus.

**Senior Minister Two**    They'll be gone before they know it.

**Senior Minister Three**    They may think they beat the Senior Ministry.

**Senior Minister Four**    But they'll be rotting in the gutter in no time.

**Senior Ministers** (*to* **Creon**)    Speaking of which –

When will we get rid of Oedipus, Creon?

Our patience is running out.

**Creon**    It's time.

**Senior Ministers**    . . . . . .?

**Creon**    Help me prepare my trip to the Oracle. It is a long way to the Temple of Hades.

**Senior Minister Two**    Not Delphi?

**Senior Minister Three**    You're seeing Tiresias at the Temple of Hades?

**Creon**    Tiresias will tell us what to do and when.

**Senior Ministers**    Creon, we put our trust in you.

**Creon**    Put your trust in the Gods. And don't utter a word about the construction being almost complete. Words can lead to undesirable outcomes. They can aggravate the already panicked people.

**Senior Ministers** *nod in agreement.*

**Creon** (*on his way out sees the* **Young Poet**)    Oh, hello there. What are you doing here?

**Young Poet**    I played the flute, as usual.

**Creon**    The flute? . . . Play it for me.

**Young Poet** *plays the flute.*

**Creon**    That's beautiful. (*Takes out a gold coin and throws it to him.*) For the tune. I have always respected artists. They are mysterious creatures, without an ounce of worldly interests. Besides, you're a different breed from those scoundrels. You have manners.

**Young Poet**    Thank you, sir.

**Creon**    The Senior Ministers are watching your friends closely. Once you get old, you forget about your youth. But don't you worry about that. I'm looking out for you. (*Exits.*)

**High Priest** (*enters*)    Zeus Almighty. Please appease your wrath and forgive us our sins. The long drought is killing us. Please send us the sweet rain of salvation and let us cultivate our lands. Tell the thunder and lightning to make it rain in Thebes.

*The* **Young Poet** *carefully bites the gold coin, as the blind* **Old Poet** *enters.*

**Old Poet**    I had never seen a gold coin before. I thought the world was just as shiny and pure as that gold coin. Of course, there were conflicts here and there. But I didn't think too much about them. I thought that's just the way it was, people would argue and then love. That's what I wanted to sing about.

**Two Poets** (*recite*)
    Oedipus –
    Oedipus –
    Oedipus –
    Someday
    A new era will dawn.

*Blackout.*

**Scene Five: The Conspiracy**

Setting: The Temple of Hades.

*Subtle scent of incense, as* **Tiresias** *recites Hesiod's Theogony[1] slowly and monotonously.*

**Tiresias**    In the beginning there was chaos. Then came Gaia, Tartarus, and Eros. Gaia gave birth to Uranus, and, with Uranus, gave birth to twelve Titans.

**Creon** *enters.*

**Tiresias**    Uranus put his twelve Titan children back into Gaia's womb, and the youngest Cronos castrated his father to death with the adamantine sickle given by his mother, and then the cosmos was ruled by one who committed patricide. Cronos married his sister Rhea, who gave birth to the Gods of Olympus, but Cronos swallowed his own children the moment they were born. He swallowed Poseidon, he swallowed Hades, he swallowed Hestia, he swallowed Demeter, he swallowed Hera, and he swallowed and swallowed and swallowed, until the youngest Zeus tricked him into vomiting them out. So he vomited Poseidon, he vomited Hades, he vomited Hestia, he vomited Hera, and he vomited and vomited and vomited, and now all the children of Cronos threw him and his brothers into the bubbling sulfur of Tartarus.

**Creon** *coughs.*

**Tiresias**    Zeus then married his sister Hera at Mount Olympus, and . . . . . . Who's there?

**Creon**    How can you foresee the future when you can't even recognize who's right in front of you?

**Tiresias**    Only a God can do both of those. Oh, it's Creon, the unfortunate one.

**Creon**    What's with the incense this late in the day?

**Tiresias**    Mosquitos. It's a hot day.

**Creon**    No one's here.

**Tiresias**    Who would come this far?

**Creon**    You sound bitter. I take it you don't enjoy being exiled.

**Tiresias**    Aren't you the one who sent me here?

**Creon**    You're blaming *me* for this? I should have listened to Jocasta who insisted I tear apart your limbs. I sent you here as a favor, as your friend.

**Tiresias**    I'm here, and you got away without even a scratch.

**Creon**    If I get a scratch, you're dead.

**Tiresias**    I thought this exile would last a year or two. Never did I expect a betrayal of our friendship.

**Creon**    The Queen is a delicate creature.

**Tiresias**    How is that witch, by the way?

**Creon**    Beautiful as ever. Sorrow enhanced her charm. She captivates the young King, just like she used to captivate you.

**Tiresias**    Queen to a young King, sounds like a good life.

**Creon**    She's in the prime of her life, having completely left behind her grief and solitude. You should see her muscles. They're firmer than a slave's. She could birth five more princes. Even ten.

*In the midst of their conversation, a faint silhouette of* **Oedipus** *and* **Jocasta** *appears.*

*Laughter.*

**Tiresias**    If only it weren't for the Sphinx. (*Smiles.*) Creon, the incredibly unfortunate one. Still no crown after two murders. The spirits of King Laius and his son must still be haunting you.

**Creon**    You should make that Creon, the fortunate one. (*Throws him a pouch filled with money.*)

**Tiresias**    . . . . . .

**Creon**    Still greedy. (*Throws him another pouch.*) It's gold. If you make this happen, I can give you ten of those.

**Tiresias**    You're desperate.

**Creon**    The people are in distress from the three-year-long drought. They are losing trust in Oedipus. A fearful crowd would do anything. They are even praying for rain, a ritual that Oedipus banned.

**Tiresias**    Rumor has it that he's bringing the water from the lake into the castle.

**Creon**    The waterway construction will be completed by the end of the year. We have to move fast. The protesters will turn back into sheep in no time. They will worship Oedipus again. Tiresias, this is our last chance to seize the throne.

**Tiresias**    What do you want me to do?

**Creon**    I need an oracle about the cause of the drought.

**Tiresias**    The cause is the weather. What else can it be? Oh, I forgot how much gold you gave me – (*Fumbles with the gold pouch.*)

**Creon**    Look, Tiresias. This is our last chance. If we succeed, we can live in prosperity for the rest of our lives.

**Tiresias**    Even without Oedipus, there are still two princes.

**Creon**    They are too young to inherit the throne. When I become regent, who's to say they will not meet the God of Death? And that's the one you serve, Hades, the God of Death, right?

**Tiresias**    Heinous fiend. Uttering such blasphemy in the sacred temple. Don't you fear the wrath of the Gods?

**Creon** *laughs*.

**Tiresias**    Stop laughing. We're in a temple, for Gods' sake. So, what do I need to do?

**Creon**    What I need from a priest is an oracle, as always. (*Laughs out loud.*)


**Scene Six: Cupid's Feast**

Setting: Inside the Castle.

**Oedipus** *(in blindfold)* and **Jocasta** *are playing a version of hide-and-seek.*

**Oedipus**    Ready or not, here I come.

**Jocasta** (*laughs*)    Catch me if you can. (*Claps.*)

**Oedipus**    Oh, I will. I hear you, and I'll get you.

**Jocasta**    No, you're not. You're sniffing at the wrong door.

**Oedipus**    Knock, knock, knock. Open the door.

**Jocasta**    Who's there?

**Oedipus**    A stranger. Open the door.

**Jocasta**    I'm eating. Get lost.

**Oedipus**    I'm dying out here. I'm getting erect. I can't wait anymore, so open the door.

**Jocasta**    Let me see. Nope, not yet. Wait until I'm finished.

**Oedipus**    That smells so good. My tummy is growling. What are you eating?

**Jocasta**    The well dried up during the drought, so I went down into it.

**Oedipus**    Alright.

**Jocasta**    At the bottom lay a white serpent, so I caught him and cooked him.

**Oedipus**    Alright, that's the smell of a serpent. I can feel it squirming now. Let me have a bite.

**Jocasta**    None for you, only for me.

**Oedipus**    If I can't bite the serpent, then I'll come for you. Let me feel your pearly, lustrous, buttery skin. Open up at once.

**Jocasta**    What a pest you are. But look at this. The door's been closed for two weeks, and I forgot how to open it.

**Oedipus**    How about like this?

*He removes his blindfold and puts his head under* **Jocasta***'s dress.* **Jocasta** *laughs her head off. They roll all over the floor ecstatically. Faint drumming sound from the* **Petitioners***.*

**Jocasta**   So, Oedipus. Tell me about yourself.

**Oedipus**   Myself? I am Oedipus. Your husband, and the King of Thebes. Previously a prince in a neighboring country. The unfortunate son, almost killed by his father because of a ridiculous oracle. But also, the fortunate one who survived all of that.

**Jocasta**   And?

**Oedipus**   A strong one. A man with firm muscles who can lift up any stone. Now tell me. How much do you love being held in these leonine arms?

**Jocasta**   I love a wise one rather than a strong one.

**Oedipus**   You got that right. I am the wisest one in Thebes. Who solved the Sphinx's riddle, which nobody could solve?

**Jocasta**   Oedipus –

**Oedipus**   Correct. Come to think of it, you are the fortunate one. You have the strongest and wisest one as your husband.

**Jocasta**   And? Tell me more.

**Oedipus**   And? . . . Human. A stupid being who plans ahead but never knows what's around the corner. Who is so insatiable that he ends up eating his own flesh and blood.

**Jocasta**   Please don't say that.

**Oedipus**   I'm kidding. I was just thinking of the Sphinx.

**Jocasta**   (*sound of drums in the distance*)   Ugh, I am so sick of those drums.

**Oedipus**   Everything will be fine once Creon comes back with the oracle.

**Jocasta**   I mean, close the window!

**Oedipus**   What made my skylark so sensitive?

**Jocasta**   Don't touch my hair! It's turning white. I said don't touch it! You're young enough to be my son . . . . . . That drumming, I'm so sick of it. It was exactly the same thirty years ago.

**Oedipus**   My Queen.

**Jocasta**   What happened before will happen again, inevitably.

**Oedipus**   . . . your hair is all over the place. Let me comb your hair. That will calm you down.

**Jocasta**   Oedipus, what if Creon comes back with bad news? That's what happened thirty years ago. The drought went on for years, the people ran out of food, and they were ready to kill. The smell of corpses filled the entire castle. People kept drumming, praying for rain. Did you have to send Creon? He's always bad news.

**Oedipus**    Who else but Creon? He's an acquaintance to both of us and the only official those nasty senior ministers respect. (*Combing her hair.*) . . . Back when I was little, my grandmother would tell me stories. In my grandmother's grandmother's grandmother's grandmother's days, the world was completely different. In place of the lineage of my father, who could not help but make enemies and fight to the death, there was the lineage of the Great Mother, who raised serpents in peace.

**Jocasta**    The lineage of the Great Mother?

**Oedipus**    There were no countries, no fathers, no houses, and no properties. No low or high, no old or young. No division between the earth and the sky. A peaceful history, with no wars. A pre-history, with only the lineage of the Great Mother . . . I miss my grandmother. The day I ran away from my father, I saw how much she cried for me. She is probably in heaven by now.

**Jocasta**    I'm going to be a grandmother soon. Look at my hair, Oedipus. Do you see? These old wrinkles and the dry white hair. . . It's terrifying. I pluck out one, and then there are two. I pluck out two, and then there are twenty. In no time it will be all white. Then nobody will see me as your wife. How about you? Will you still love me?

**Oedipus**    Oh, that's why you are so sensitive. If you are this crabby over a couple of white hairs, you'll drive me insane when all you have is white hair. What do I do? Upon sunrise, I will issue a decree on Thebes. Dark-haired women shall not leave the house. The punishment upon violation will be shaving their head.

**Jocasta**    Oh, Oedipus! (*Laughs.*)

**Oedipus**    Now you're laughing. Making you laugh is as hard as gathering water during a drought.

**Jocasta**    . . . . . . My King. You are the first to bring sunshine to my exhausted life. You are my reason for being. We will share a grave, which will be our sanctuary. I will never let you go. So, Oedipus, don't ever desert me.

*The drumming outside gets louder, and the murmuring of the* **Petitioners** *continue.*

*Blackout.*


**Scene Seven: In Between the Stories**

Setting: After the Feast.

*The* **Old Poet** *is putting the musical instruments and puppets away as* **Boy** *enters.*

**Boy** *throws him a piece of bread.*

**Old Poet**    Are they all gone?

**Boy**   They wouldn't leave, not until you were done. They were completely immersed in your story.

**Old Poet**   We had nice wind today. Nice rosemary scent. A perfect day for a song.

**Boy**   The wind comes from the Colonus Forest. It's the sweetest at this time of the year . . . . . . You've been all around the world, right? Then have you seen the fanatics following Dionysus? People say that they get drunk and sing and dance along the beach on the southern island.

**Old Poet**   I think I've heard of them. There is supposedly a drunk God who is unlike any other ruthless and omnipotent God, who eats and drinks, and laughs and cries with the people, like a fool.

**Boy**   They're witches. I hear they *make* people laugh and cry, and if they don't like them, they tear them to pieces. . . . . . My father says you are a follower of Dionysus. Do you bewitch people with your stories?

**Old Poet**   . . . . . .

**Boy**   Last fall on threshing day, some storytellers came to our town and sang about Oedipus. Why is their story different from yours?

**Old Poet**   Because we are different storytellers.

**Boy**   But the stories are completely different. In their version, Oedipus is a monster in human shape, but in yours, he is not that at all. And the more I listen to you, the more I believe your story. Since your story bewitches me, you must be a witch. You're Dionysus in disguise!

**Old Poet** *laughs*.

**Boy**   Weird old man. (*Picks up the bread from the ground.*) Eat this. You were too busy singing to eat anything.

**Old Poet**   Thank you. But young master, it's about time for me to leave. Also, your father must be worried –

**Boy**   No way! You didn't finish your Oedipus story. As long as you sing, customers will keep coming. My father will be happy with the money they bring. . . . . . (*He points at a puppet.*) Is this Creon?

**Old Poet** *takes out the puppet the* **Boy** *points at.*

**Boy**   Can I touch him? (*Shyly takes the puppet and imitates the* **Old Poet**.) After Creon receives the oracle from the blind prophet Tiresias, he heads back to Thebes. (*Loosens the puppet strings and recites in the manner of the* **Old Poet**.)
Here I come, here I come, here I come.
Back to the sick old Thebes. . . . . .

*Stops reciting.*

Your story makes these puppets feel so alive. Last fall, Oedipus was an ugly devil, but now I'm beginning to like him. Am I really bewitched? At some point, my heart is pounding, and I can't stop crying, and I am hiding behind customers so that my father can't see me cry. But this can't be right, since Oedipus is a bad guy.

**Old Poet**    This is just a story.

**Boy**    So it's all lies? There is no real Oedipus?

**Old Poet**    Real Oedipus, hmm.

*He stoops to the* **Boy***'s height and points at his mouth and the* **Boy***'s ear.*

**Old Poet**    Might be somewhere here? In between the stories. Somewhere between the right ear and the left ear?

**Boy**    Crazy old man. May Dionysus take down your gross drunken ass.

**Old Poet** (*laughs*)    What I say is true. Some stories are easily perceived by the ears, and some stories exist in between the lines. Only people with keen ears can hear the hidden stories and be touched by them. That's what happens when the truth in the hidden stories comes to life.

**Boy**    Yes, I felt that. My heart was beating.

**Old Poet**    That means you have keen ears. Some ears have chains around them and only absorb unnecessary stories. Others are blocked with a stone, so stories, no matter how good, can't get through. That's why every story in the world needs to be smooth and slick.

**Boy**    My ears don't have chains. Some earwax, maybe. Let's go in. I hid a bottle of wine on the kitchen cupboard just for you. (*He looks back on his way out. He picks up the puppet on the ground and sits it up.*) Creon! Wait here . . . When I was little, I thought puppets were alive. I thought that, when we went to sleep or went out, all the puppets in the neighborhood would climb out of the chimney or jump out the window and gather and have their secret meeting and not tell us about it. (*He holds the* **Old Poet***'s hand and jumps excitedly.*) I thought that was just my childhood imagination. But I guess it could be the hidden story you're talking about.

### Scene Eight: Interlude

Setting: An Empty Stage.

**Creon** *enters on one side.*

*There is a scorching sun in the middle of the sky, and there is a window under the sun.*

**Macbeth**, *a man in medieval knight costume, enters through the window.*

*They both move like puppets.*

**Macbeth**
"If it were done when 'tis done, then 'twere well
It were done quickly: if th'assassination

Could trammel up the consequence, and catch
With his surcease success; that but this blow
Might be the be-all and the end-all—here,
But here, upon this bank and shoal of time,
We'd jump the life to come.—But in these cases,
We still have judgment here; that we but teach
Bloody instructions, which, being taught, return
To plague th'inventor: this even-handed Justice
Commends th'ingredience of our poison'd chalice
To our own lips. He's here in double trust:
First, as I am his kinsman and his subject,
Strong both against the deed:"[2]

**Creon**   Halt, stranger. Your outfit is peculiar, and your words suspicious. Who are you to climb through the window?

**Macbeth**   Macbeth.

**Creon**   Who?

**Macbeth**   Macbeth from Scotland. I live next door.

**Creon**   Scotland? Odd name. This is Thebes, governed by Oedipus.

**Macbeth**   Thebes? *That* Thebes? Governed by *that* Oedipus? In ancient Greece?

**Creon**   Yes. We are performing *Oedipus the King*.

**Macbeth**   No way. I just got lost in the forest and, no way.

**Creon**   What are you doing here?

**Macbeth**   I saw this window. And, well, what am I doing here? I'm afraid I am in the wrong play. . . . . . But are you sure this is Thebes? Could you maybe be wrong, and could this be Scotland?

**Creon**   Could be. The sun is scorching, and I've lost all sense of direction.

**Macbeth**   That sun is really something. It's so bright and sweltering that my head is getting numb. Singing and dancing under this sun can easily make you want to jump off a cliff. Well, what does it matter *where* we are? Truth is always going to be out there, where it is unreachable and ungraspable. Anyway, did you by any chance encounter King Duncan on your way?

**Creon**   To find King Duncan, you should look through the plays of Shakespeare. I'm looking for Oedipus. Where am I? I'm completely lost. Where the hell is the playwright? She should advance the plot.

**Macbeth**   Who knows? Probably meandering around somewhere. But look, . . . what do we do if our destinies get switched? It's possible that I will find King Oedipus instead of King Duncan, and you will encounter King Duncan.

**Creon**   That's right. So we must find the playwright immediately. (*He is fidgety, and then gets an idea.*) Oh. I have an idea. How about you play Creon, and I play Macbeth?

**Macbeth**    Brilliant. So it's as though you're changing the wheels of a carriage, but the carriage will keep on its course. For that witty solution, I will give you a piece of advice in return. It's about your expression. From the intense determination on your face, I can see that you are on to something big. I suggest you put on a different mask. Otherwise, the whole world will keep its eyes on you.

**Creon** (*slowly touches his face*)    Do I look that suspicious? I wish I had a mirror.

**Macbeth**    You do. The whole world is our mirror. (*Points at the auditorium.*) There, and there. (*Points to a male audience member.*) Let me see, the right face for you is that one. Look at him closely. Inside, he's a complete snake, but that gentle smile and tranquil gaze make it look as if he has no worldly interests. Hmmm—what a disguise. (*Takes out a pair of sunglasses from his pocket and hands them to* **Creon**.) My gift for you. They'll come in handy.

**Creon** (*exiting*)    Thank you, my friend. In return, I'm giving you my blessing. (*Putting on the sunglasses.*) . . . Hail Macbeth. Macbeth will rule Scotland. Macbeth will be King of Scotland.

**Macbeth**
    Shush! That's a secret . . . . .
    "Now o'er the one-half world
    Nature seems dead, and wicked dreams abuse
    The curtain'd sleep: Witchcraft celebrates
    Pale Hecate's off'rings; and wither'd Murther,
    Alarum'd by his sentinel, the wolf,
    Whose howl's his watch, thus with his stealthy pace,
    With Tarquin's ravishing strides, towards his design
    Moves like a ghost.—Thou sure and firm-set earth,
    Hear not my steps, which way they walk, for fear
    Thy very stones prate of my where-abouts,
    And take the present horror from the time,
    Which now suits with it."[3]

**Macbeth** *walks directly into the auditorium.*

*He draws his sword.*

*Blackout.*


**Scene Nine: The Ceremony of Massacre**

Setting: In Front of the Gates of Thebes.

*Sun is still scorching.*

*Gathering of* **Citizens of Thebes***, exhausted from the drought.*

*In one corner the* **Old Poet** *is either manipulating the puppet or playing the flute.*

**Citizen One**    Hey, one bucket per household.

**Citizen Two**    You there, you count as one household. Why are you taking two buckets when everybody else is taking one?

**Citizen Three**    Your accusation is appalling. I'm doing no such thing. My first one was just half a bucket. Everybody saw it.

**Citizen Two**    I'm not buying it. Return the second bucket.

**Citizen Three**    Hey, you're not the King. Don't order me around.

**Citizen Two**    Who are *you* to tell me what to do? I'm gonna kick your ass.

**Citizen Three**    Fine. Just kill me now. I'm dying of thirst anyway. But with King Oedipus back, you will pay for your offense. Now what happened to that ass-kicking you were talking about?

**Citizen Two**    The heat messed you up real bad. Be careful what you ask for. (*They fight and knock over a bucket of water.*) Oh, my water! What do I do? This is for my whole family.

**Citizen One**    To appease the wrath of the Gods, we must offer a woman as a sacrifice, like in the olden days.

**Citizen Three**    How about your daughter?

**Citizen Two**    What an ass. Shut your mouth or I'll rip out your tongue.

**Citizen Three**    I'll shoot your eyes with fire arrows first.

**Citizen Two**    I curse you that you will not see a single drop of rain for the rest of your life.

**Citizen Three**    I curse you that you will choke to death on rain.

*The* **Citizens of Thebes** *get into a physical fight.*

*The castle gate opens, and* **Oedipus** *enters with* **Jocasta**.

*Silence.*

**Old Poet** (*recites*)
    Oedipus, Oedipus
    Thebes is burning.
    Burning up like sulfur.
    Oedipus, Oedipus
    Save Thebes from this curse
    Like you saved Thebes from the Sphinx.

**Oedipus**    The suffering of the people of Thebes is also my suffering. Citizens of Thebes, worry no more. I sent out Creon to receive an oracle, and he will return today with good news. (*Trumpet sound.*) Oh, the trumpets. Creon's back.

*The* **Old Poet** *plays the flute.*

*The* **Citizens of Thebes** *freeze like wax dolls, in anticipation of* **Creon** *and the oracle.*

*Silence.*

**Creon** *and* **Tiresias** *enter.*

**Jocasta** *screams.*

**Tiresias**    That voice. Is that Jocasta, the beautiful Queen of my dreams?

**Jocasta**    I thought you were dead!

**Creon**    Sister, what a blasphemous thing to say to the noble Priest delivering the oracle. . . Your Majesty, this is Priest Tiresias, who's been looking over Thebes for a long time. He may be blind, but he can see what nobody else can see, the future and our destiny. This wise man will deliver the oracle personally.

**Jocasta**    What use is this sightless freak in the world of the seeing?

**Oedipus**    Calm down, My Queen. People are waiting to hear the oracle.

**Jocasta**    This is a curse, My King. This man – (*Suddenly, she grabs* **Tiresias***' hands.*) No, Divine Priest. I forgive you for all of your sins. So please stop torturing me and give me your blessings. Please don't inflict any more pain on me, like you did before.

**Tiresias**    My Queen, we're only human. How can we escape the pain the Gods inflict upon us? (*Kisses* **Jocasta***'s hand.*) Dear Gods, why did you gift me with the ability to see the future, when we live in a world where wisdom is useless?

**Oedipus**    Creon. What kind of an oracle is so nonsensical and incoherent?

**Creon**    It is an oracle about the exile of a person, or—it is about paying blood with blood. But more than that, I cannot say. Perhaps we should talk inside the castle.

**Citizens of Thebes**    Creon, what nonsense is this? Don't hide anything from us. We deserve to hear the oracle word for word.

**Jocasta**    Who is this person you're talking about? Is the oracle concerning our child?

**Creon**    Sister, I really cannot say more.

**Oedipus**    The fate of Thebes is contingent upon this oracle. Creon, what does the oracle say?

**Citizens of Thebes**    Tell us the truth, Creon. Deliver the oracle.

**Tiresias**    It concerns the Queen's child, but not the King's.

**Oedipus**    Don't be cryptic. Just spit it out.

**Tiresias**    Then let me be the messenger of the Divine Will. (*The* **Citizens** *gather around* **Creon** *and* **Tiresias**.) The oracle says that the murderer of King Laius is currently in Thebes. The Gods are enraged because this man has not been punished for his sins.

**Jocasta**    Oh, there's a glimmer of hope. My King, the priest is talking about the murder of King Laius by a band of thieves during his trip abroad about ten years ago. Back then the tyranny of the Sphinx was enough trouble, and we could not give attention to finding the real culprit. But punishing us now for what happened ten years ago is spiteful, especially for Gods.

**Oedipus**    Does the oracle say who the murderer is?

**Tiresias**    Please don't dig any deeper. You may fall into the hole and break a leg.

**Oedipus**    Wise sir, the long drought led to famine, and people are starving to death. Don't overlook the suffering of Thebes, and give us the name of the murderer.

**Tiresias**    Why would you, finite being, want to dig up the distant past, when you can't even deal with the present? This will only bring you harm. This oracle is better left undisturbed.

**Oedipus** (*drawing his sword*)    How insolent!

**Tiresias**    Well, well—This rash being is digging his own grave.

**Creon**    Your Majesty, there is a reason for his discretion.

**Oedipus**    No reason or exception can be justified to keep us from saving Thebes. Who is the murderer?

**Tiresias**    Someone of noble status.

**Oedipus**    In Thebes, every crime is punishable by law, regardless of the culprit's class or status. That's Oedipus' law.

**Tiresias**    It is also someone of noble character.

**Oedipus**    A noble character murders the King and walks around freely? Don't waste our time and give us the name. Creon, I order *you* to answer.

**Creon**    Do I really have to?

**Oedipus**    It's the King's command.

**Creon**    He is among us right here.

**Citizens of Thebes** (*recite, whispering with alarm*)
  Who the devil can this be,
  Committing such a heinous crime
  And living among us shamelessly?
  Creon, do let us know!
  We'll tear him apart from limb to limb,
  Cut out his bloody heart,
  And feed it to the hungry crows.
  The cause of our dried-up wells
  Incites our appetite for justice.
  Who the devil can this be?

**Creon**    Someone who killed his father and slept with his mother.

*Silence.*

*Sound of light thunder.*

**Oedipus** (*aside*)   What's this I hear? Everybody's gone dead silent all of a sudden. I feel something ominous in the air. A priest told me the same tale ten years ago. It can't be. That oracle circulated all over Greece. It even made King Laius kill his own son. Moreover, I am innocent.

**Creon**   Citizens of Thebes, I seek your advice. Should I arrest this person, who is of noble status, a dear friend of mine, who has devoted his life to Thebes?

**Tiresias**   Creon, it should be done for Thebes.

**Creon**   For Thebes?

**Citizens of Thebes**   For Thebes.

**Creon**   Very well. Senior Ministers, draw your swords. Block the roads. We are arresting the murderer.

*Sound of* **Senior Ministers** *drawing their swords.*

**Citizens** *stand still yet vigilant like hungry wolves.*

**Creon**   The murderer of King Laius is, and I swear this on my grave, . . . . . . King Oedipus. Arrest him.

*The stage turns into shock-filled chaos. People scream. Soldiers with weapons surround* **Oedipus***. The* **Young Poet** *and some* **Young People** *sense the danger and step aside.*

**Young Person One**   Everybody's gone insane. The drought destroyed the Spirit of Thebes.

**Young Person Two**   Stop.

**Young Person Three**   If we stay here, we'll die for nothing.

**Young Person Two**   We must save Oedipus.

**Young Person Four**   The tide has turned. Let's convene at the tavern at dawn tomorrow.

**Young Poet**   I'm a mere poet. I've never even touched a sword.

**Young Person Two** (*grabbing the* **Young Poet**)   If we don't help Oedipus, nobody will.

**Young Person Two** *pushes the timid* **Young Poet** *into the crowd of* **Young People**.

**Old Poet**   That's right, I'm a mere poet. Singing and telling stories, that's all I can do. Sharing beautiful stories with the world, that's all I've ever wanted. About kindness. About love. The wind. The sky. The universe. Children laughing. A woman's skin. Liquor and the river. About the wrinkles of time and deep friendship . . . There was nothing else I could do in that bloody, corrupt world. I could merely watch.

**Oedipus**    "Oh riches, oh power. Talent that exceeds all other talents in the competition of life. How tenacious is the jealousy that attaches to you all. Because of the crown this city bestowed upon me, my dear and loyal friend Creon is now scheming to get rid of me and has recruited as his co-conspirator that impostor of a prophet who only sees profit but cannot see the future."[4] . . . This is treason. I am Oedipus, King of Thebes.

**Tiresias**    Creon delivered exactly what the oracle says.

**Creon**    Take him away. His beastly outburst is a clear sign of his admission of guilt. (**Oedipus** *is taken away.*)

**Jocasta**    Creon, this is outrageous.

**Creon**    For Thebes, this had to be done.

**Jocasta**    You are my flesh and blood. You're Oedipus' brother-in-law.

**Creon**    And his uncle.

**Jocasta**    . . . What are you talking about?

**Creon**    It's true, sister. Oedipus is your own son whom we all thought died thirty years ago.

**Jocasta**    . . . . . .

**Creon**    When we handed Oedipus to the shepherd, we all believed he would die. But the Gods work in ways we mere mortals can hardly comprehend. To teach us a lesson in humility, the Gods spared Oedipus' life, like a miracle, and had him murder his father and sleep with his mother, just as the oracle says.

**Jocasta**    My son is dead. You killed him with your own hands thirty years ago. You're lying!

**Creon**    How could I kill my own flesh and blood? I told King Laius that I killed him to avoid his wrath. But the truth is I ordered a shepherd to take the baby deep into the forest and leave him there. That way I thought he would die on his own.

**Jocasta**    You're saying he's alive? I didn't even get to breastfeed him, and he's been alive all this time?

**Creon**    Indeed.

**Tiresias**    This is all in the Gods' design. How can we, mere humans, understand the way of the Gods? We can only bow our heads in humility.

**Jocasta**    Why do the Gods interfere with humans? What have they against me?

**Young Person Two**    My Queen, don't fall for such blasphemy! This is treason. Please keep yourself together.

**Creon**    Arrest him too. He defends the murderer. Citizens of Thebes, I declare an emergency. Anyone who disobeys my order, anyone who rebels and disrupts the peace and order in Thebes, will be punished immediately. (*Sound of a siren. The* **Young Poet** *and the remaining* **Young People** *run away.* **Creon** *puts on the sunglasses he received from* **Macbeth**.) . . . . . . Thebes is in utter shock from learning that their beloved King turned out to be a criminal unprecedented in human history. I am deeply saddened to learn about this myself. For your consolation, today you can collect five buckets of water per household from the well at the castle gate.

**Petitioners**    Water? Hail Creon, hail Thebes!

*The* **Petitioners** *gather around the well.*

**Petitioners** (*recite*)
    Hail, Creon!
    He gives us water, he gives us blood.
    Who cares who's king
    As long as he gives us
    A bucket of water to quench our thirst,
    A feast of blood to wet our appetite?
    Gods in heaven, how fair they are.
    In place of rain, they pour us blood.
    Once upon a time, back in the day,
    There was a wise man
    Who solved the riddles of the Sphinx.
    But he kneels, defeated
    By the incomprehensible oracle.
    Why would you humans look beyond
    The narrow expanse of your view?
    To be finite is to be human.
    Hail, Creon.
    Let the blood rain down on Thebes.
    May a downpour of blood end the drought.

**Jocasta** (*her hair has turned completely white*)    My husband is my son, and my children are the children of my son. Laius, are you watching this? Your revenge is out of this world.

*While the* **Petitioners** *recite, the* **Young People** *are getting hanged. The* **Petitioners** *and* **Citizens** *stop their singing and dancing and look at* **Jocasta**. *They approach* **Jocasta** *like wolves approach prey or like vigilantes approach a pariah.* **Jocasta** *stumbles back. Then she stops, frozen like a cornered mouse.*

**Jocasta**    Laius, is this your curse? You really couldn't bear to see me happy, even though you never made me so. Fine. Now see this. Me being torn apart. Enjoy, you and your merciless Gods! Laius –!

*She opens her arms to the wolves.*

*Blackout.*

**Scene Ten: Survivor's Sorrow**

*The body of* **Young Person Two** *is hanging in the air.*

**Old Poet** *approaches him.*

**Old Poet** *takes off his shoes and puts them on* **Young Person Two**.

**Old Poet** *looks at* **Young Person Two** *and hugs his legs.*

*Silence.*


**Scene Eleven: Rise and Fall**

*On one side of the wall are shadows of the hanged bodies.*

*Underneath is a faint image of* **Oedipus** *in jail.*

*The stage is* **Creon**'s *office.*

**Creon** *and* **Tiresias**.

**Creon** *hands a box to* **Tiresias**.

**Tiresias** (*takes out a pin from the box and touches it*)    It's an ornament. Gold?

**Creon**    It was on Jocasta's garment. Keep it as a relic.

**Tiresias**    Did you give her a good burial?

**Creon**    She threw herself off the cliff, so her body's torn to pieces. The furious citizens chased her like hungry wolves. I was fond of her. We couldn't have been more different from each other, even when we were little. (*Sheds a tear.*) No, I can't give in to sadness and weakness. The moment I've been dreaming about for decades has finally arrived. This is all for Thebes. (*Blows his nose.*) If only it would rain now.

**Tiresias**    Rain. . . But be careful, Creon. When it rains, everyone will rejoice for a moment. They will all be on your side. But the rain can also wake them up and wash away the blood. When that happens, everything you've been dreaming about for decades can vanish.

**Creon**    The rain can wake them up?

**Tiresias**    No need to panic, Creon. That's why I'm here. I've got it all figured out.

**Creon**    What will you do?

**Tiresias**    A story. . . . . . A story that frames Oedipus on all counts. When that spreads, everyone will forget that Oedipus is the King of Kings. A grand epic will do that. Possibly one that will teach the citizens of Thebes a moral lesson.

**Creon**    Replace the Oedipus in reality with the Oedipus in the story? Not bad. What should we call it? *The Secret of Thebes*, *The Curse of the Sphinx* . . . No, the title should have Oedipus in it. Since he's the hero of the story. *Oedipus, the Immoral King*?

**Tiresias**   Don't you find it unjust? I know it's just a story. But does it still have to be all about him?

**Creon**   I am a humble person, Tiresias. If there is one thing I would like for myself, it is that the Creon in the story is nobler than the Creon in reality. Just a little bit. And make yourself the world's most prominent prophet. The very best.

*They laugh.*

**Tiresias** *screams.*

**Tiresias**   Ow! The pin pricked me.

**Creon** (*laughs*)   That's Jocasta's revenge.

**Tiresias** (*returns the pin*)   Take it back.

**Creon**   Aw, did that hurt so much?

**Tiresias**   It's of no use to a blind person. Give it back to Oedipus.

**Creon**   Not a bad idea. After the trial, maybe I'll poke out his eyes with this. (*Laughs.*) Oh, how about this, Tiresias? We can give you eyesight in our new epic.

**Tiresias**   Eyesight? I've been blind my whole life. What does it matter whether I have eyesight or not in our story? What I'm thinking is making Apollo the God of my temple. In a grand epic, Apollo, the God of light, would fit better than Hades, the God of death.

**Creon**   Then the new temple we're building for you can be dedicated to Apollo as well.

**Tiresias**   How magnanimous. Noble Creon, it's true that power makes one unselfish.

*They laugh.*

*In a scenic transition,* **Oedipus'** *space lights up.*

**Oedipus** *and* **Young Poet** *have jail bars between them.*

**Young Poet**   Nobody showed up at the rendezvous. All my friends are corpses hanging there like flags. Regrettably, I'm the only survivor.

**Oedipus**   Then you are my only hope.

**Young Poet**   I am no hope, Your Majesty.

**Oedipus**   . . . . . . Run. The trial will begin soon, so while all eyes are on me, you should escape. Run away and sing your songs again. Sing about justice.

**Young Poet**   There is no justice left on earth. No more light, no more hope.

**Oedipus**   Then wait until you can sing again. When you do, sing about me so the world will know my story.

**Young Poet**  . . . . . .

**Guard**  It's time to go. My shift is up soon. (*Holds out his hand.*) You have that gold coin you promised me? If not, I can make you stay here.

**Young Poet** (*throws him the gold coin*)   There. Take that dirty coin, which belonged to Creon.

**Oedipus**  Don't be stupid. Run. And sing your song.

*Sound of wind.*

**Young Poet**  How am I supposed to sing after escaping like a coward? When you are still behind bars? No, you are the cause of all this. You should have been wiser. You should have eliminated your enemies completely or made peace with them. That would have made all of us happy. Justice has no place on this earth. . . . . . Then why is this so painful? What can I sing about? Praising evil? The shame of surviving? Or the greed of those hiding behind a mask? The immoral act of sleeping with the enemy? Envy, uncontrollable like an aggressive cat? Violence and lies? Betrayal and antagonism? What is the fate of this story?


**Scene Twelve: The Revenge of the Sphinx**

*The* **Guard** *hands* **Oedipus** *food.*

**Oedipus** *eats slowly.*

**Guard**  The human of humans, the King of Kings is now imprisoned in the sewer. Eat up. Once the trial begins, your life will be puny. . . . . . Oedipus, the being who will eat and eat until he eats his own flesh, the fool who plans ahead but never knows what's around the corner. What's the riddle? Four legs in the morning, two in the afternoon. (*Exits laughing.*)

**Oedipus** (*jumps up and pounds on the iron bars*)   That's Human. Show yourself, Sphinx. You were right all along. Now it's my turn to walk on three legs. Bring the cane, Sphinx! Let me show you the end of a helpless, defeated human. . . No, Sphinx. Actually, your spell didn't work. Look at my friends. Before walking on three legs, they all became birds and flew away. . . My brave friends, I am so lonely I feel inclined to believe you are still alive. Don't just hang there and laugh without me. Talk to me. What does the world look like from up above? How is our precious Thebes we all tried to protect? For what did you all sacrifice your youth? Damn this reform we gave our lives to. Damn this ideal. . . . . . I am lonely.

*The stage lights up. The sound of fanfare, as* **Creon** *and the* **Senior Ministers** *enter.*

*The stage is a courtroom.*

**Senior Minister One**  The trial is in session. The defendant is Oedipus, King of Thebes. On the surface, he is the wise man who solved the riddle of the Sphinx, but inside he violated Divine Providence by sharing a bed with his mother after killing his father. What is the crime we didn't know about, and what is the hidden truth?

**Senior Minister Two**    I request Creon as a witness. To the stand! Do you swear to tell the truth, the whole truth, and nothing but the truth, so help me God?

**Creon**    I do.

**Senior Minister Three**    Did you receive an order from King Laius to kill his son thirty years ago?

**Creon**    That's the truth, I swear.

**Senior Minister Two**    What did you do with the child?

**Creon**    I ordered a servant to take him away to a neighboring country. Fortunately, the servant is still alive so he can verify my statement.

**Senior Minister One**    Second witness, to the stand!

**Old Man One** *comes out with a cunning yet fawning demeanor.*

**Senior Minister Two**    Identify yourself.

**Old Man One**    I am a servant to Master Creon. Yes, sir, I am. This is no lie. I only tell the truth.

**Senior Minister Three**    Thirty years ago, did you receive an order from Creon to take away a child?

**Old Man One**    I sure did, sir. Master Creon handed me a child wrapped in a silk quilt. I tell no lies. He said to me, "Don't kill him but sneak him out and take him away." So I snuck out at night and gave the child to a shepherd in a neighboring country.

**Senior Minister Three**    After that, did you hear about the child?

**Old Man One**    Not just hear. I went over to see him myself. I'm telling the truth, sir. I am not one to tell a lie. While I was out herding my sheep, I ran into the shepherd. He told me that his King, who was childless, took him in as a stepson. So I went there and took a look at him from a distance, to see how he was doing.

**Senior Minister Two**    Do you remember the child's face?

**Old Man One**    I sure do. It was thirty years ago, but it's clear as day. He was not just a handsome devil but a mirror image of King Laius. It's the truth, sir. I swear I'm only telling the truth. I remember his face so well I can draw it right now. Yes, sir.

**Senior Minister Three**    Since you remember him so well, tell us whether he has any resemblance with the arrested Oedipus.

**Old Man One**    More than resemblance, sir. They look exactly the same. I never shared this with anyone. But when I first laid eyes on King Oedipus, I recognized him at once as the very child. Same eyes, same nose. Exactly the same. It's the truth, sir. I never told a lie in my whole life. Master Creon can tell you how loyal a servant I am. Never in my life have I disobeyed Master Creon's orders. If he says drop dead, I'll drop . . . Not that he ever gave me such an order. Considering that I am still alive.

**Senior Minister Three**    Enough. Stop talking and step down.

**Senior Minister One**    It has been revealed that Oedipus is the son of former King Laius. Now we will verify the oracle that he killed his own father. Third witness!

**Old Man Two** *enters timidly.*

**Senior Minister One**    Identify yourself.

**Old Man Two**    I, I am herding sheep in the mountain, but I used to be the stableman in the castle.

**Senior Minister Three**    Tell us what happened ten years ago.

**Old Man Two**    Ten years ago, when King Laius was visiting the neighboring country, I was his stableman. We encountered a band of thieves on the road.

**Senior Minister Two**    You mean one thief, not a band of them.

**Old Man Two** (*trembling with fear*)    Yes, sir.

**Senior Minister Three**    Continue.

**Old Man** *hesitates.*

**Senior Minister Four**    We said continue.

**Old Man Two**    I left the castle in a hurry and am now herding sheep in the mountain.

**Senior Minister Two**    What are you talking about? What does sheep have to do with thieves?

**Old Man Two**    Well, the thing is . . . Sirs, please forgive this poor old soul. Since you cut me off, I forgot the turn of events. I spent all night memorizing it, but my old brain cannot keep up.

**Senior Minister Two**    . . . . . .

**Tiresias**    That's what old age does, it makes you forget things. Since he is an old man, let him tell his story without cutting him off.

**Senior Minister One**    Well then. Start from the beginning.

**Old Man Two** (*as if reading a book*)    Now I am herding sheep in the mountain, but I used to be the stableman in the castle. Ten years ago, when King Laius was visiting the neighboring country, I was his stableman. We encountered a band of . . . I mean, one thief on the road, and he stole our gold and killed King Laius. All five guards died, and I was the only survivor. When I returned to Thebes, that mur–, murderer was King. I got scared, so I left the castle in a hurry and am now herding sheep in the mountain.

**Senior Minister Three**    Take a close look. Is the man behind bars the murderer?

**Old Man Two**    . . . I am certain he is.

**Senior Minister One**    Lastly, we have witnesses who will testify to the fitness of Oedipus as ruler.

*The* **Young People** *who used to follow* **Oedipus** *enter.*

**Oedipus** *stands up.*

**Senior Minister Two**    With the backing of the King, you rascals frequented the tavern and got drunk and acted recklessly, when the citizens of Thebes were suffering from the scorching heat. But Thebes is lenient. To you, entitled and insolent lot, we offer you a chance to tell the truth. Tell us about the *real* King Oedipus,

**Young Person One**    King Oedipus is . . . (*Hesitates.*)

**Senior Minister Three**    We said speak!

**Young Person Three**    King Oedipus stole taxes.

**Senior Minister One**    Louder.

**Young People** (*frantically*)    King Oedipus never had a construction project. There is no lake outside the castle. Oedipus is a hypocrite! Citizens, Oedipus is a shameless criminal!

**Oedipus** (*shaking the iron bars*)    Liars!

*Blackout.*

### Scene Thirteen: The Song of the Young Poet

*There is a sound of wind amid the silence.*

*Lights on. The entrance of the Colonus Forest.*

**Boy** *and* **Old Poet**.

**Boy**    Creon stabbed his eyes with a needle? That's horrifying. (*Sighs.*) So the blind Oedipus settled here?

**Old Poet**    Here in Colonus Forest. Apparently, he and his daughter Antigone went in together.

**Boy**    . . . . . . I heard that Poseidon's horse once lived in this divine forest. Then there was a terrifying goddess who took revenge and showed benevolence. I wonder what Oedipus is thinking in there.

**Old Poet**    The moon is so bright. I suppose the clouds will soon cover the moon.

**Boy**    Old man, I think . . . No, tell me another story. The glimmering moonlight is making me crave another story.

**Old Poet**    Since you mentioned a horse living in this forest, let me tell you about Pegasus, Poseidon's flying horse. (*Plays the flute.*) Upon entering the Peloponnese Peninsula, you reach Corinth, a city that worships Aphrodite. There is a spring there, which was created when Pegasus kicked off the ground to fly. The spring is the source of poetry. If you drink from that spring, inspiration pours out and makes you the greatest poet.

**Boy**    The greatest poet?

**Old Poet**    A man named Bellerophon tamed the Pegasus. He acquired Athena's reins through good fortune, mounted Pegasus, and flew around. (*Plays a flute tune like ascending into the sky.*) He must have thought he was a God. One day he became so arrogant that he rode Pegasus without putting on the reins, right up the sky. Zeus was watching. He frowned and snapped his fingers, and Bellerophon fell to the ground, becoming blind and crippled.

**Boy**    And the Spring of Corinth?

**Old Poet**    It was created that day when Pegasus had kicked off the ground to fly without its reins.

**Boy**    You said that spot is the source of poetry? Even when he became blind and crippled?

**Old Poet**    Well, he still saw a world nobody has ever seen and flew around Zeus' sky . . . In the Temple of Delphi, they teach *meden agan*,[5] to do nothing in excess. Poetry might be the exact opposite . . . Do everything in excess.

**Boy**    You drank from that spring yourself. Is that why your story is so captivating, more than any other story? . . . The Spring of Corinth . . . . Old man, I have a confession to make.

**Old Poet**    . . . . . .

**Boy**    I'm thinking of leaving home. I'm all grown up now, you know. When you go in there, into the Colonus Forest, I'll have no more joy left. I can't breathe next to my father. I want to see the world. You've seen a lot of the world, right? Come with me. People say that there are ghosts in the Colonus Forest, so you can go in, but nobody comes out.

**Old Poet**    Where do you want to go?

**Boy**    First, to Corinth to drink from that spring. Then see the world . . . and finally, Naxos.

**Old Poet**    Naxos?

**Boy** (*nods*)    The island of Dionysus. They welcome anyone there. All they do is drink, dance, and sing. They wear these masks, and the masks possess you, so if you wear an eagle's mask, you become an eagle . . . The transformation is so fascinating that even the spectators act like eagles and laugh and cry and go crazy.

**Old Poet**    I see. I think I heard a tale like that myself. The song and dance are so enchanting that cold-hearted people open their hearts and laugh and cry together, even with their enemies.

**Boy**    So come with me, old man. Nobody enters this forest. It's keeping its mouth shut, like it's angry or something.

**Old Poet**    On a full moon like tonight, they say the forest reveals its path.

**Boy**    Nonsense. I heard the forest reveals its path when it's completely dark. How can it be completely dark when there is a full moon? It's all made up.

**Old Poet**    But Oedipus went into the forest.

**Boy**    Oedipus is blind. It's always dark for him, whether the moon is full or new.

**Old Poet**    . . . That makes sense. (*Sighs.*)

**Boy**    Stop wasting time and let's go. Since the forest is keeping its mouth shut, it looks like the goddess of vengeance doesn't like our presence. I heard she has a monstrous look.

**Old Poet**    Go on your own, young master.

**Boy**    Stubborn old man. Get lost then. I hope the goddess of vengeance snatches up your ungrateful ass. (*Gets up.*) What a waste of time. It's scary going back alone at night!

**Old Poet** (*laughs and hands him the flute*)    Play this while you walk.

**Boy**    What?

**Old Poet**    The flute.

**Boy**    Why are you giving this to me?

**Old Poet**    You wanted to have it.

**Boy**    This is precious. If you give it to me, how are you going to sing?

**Old Poet**    I can barely sing at this old age. My whole life, I thought singing would make my hopes come true . . . but I've sung enough. I'd like to spend the rest of my life quietly in the Colonus Forest.

**Boy**    Then . . . shall I sing?

**Old Poet**    What a brilliant idea. If you sing, then the story will continue even in my absence.

**Boy**    Can I . . . also become a poet?

**Old Poet**    Certainly.

**Boy**    People say that I have quite a good voice. I remember all the songs you sang. From now on you are my master . . . . . . I mean it. I remember every one of your songs word for word. I have the best memory in this town. I will sing your version of the Oedipus story everyday, instead of the version people are familiar with. When I have children, I will sing it to them, and then to their children, too. So even when you are gone, your story will continue to live. But . . . can I change a few verses? Your story is too sad and scary. May I, change it just a little bit?

**Old Poet** *nods*.

**Boy**    Really? If my story replaces your story, will that be okay?

**Old Poet**    That . . . is the fate of the story.

**Boy**    I promise. I will keep singing your song and will portray Oedipus more beautifully. I will keep singing so that Oedipus will not be forgotten. (*Filled with emotion,* **Boy** *hugs the* **Old Poet**.)

**Old Poet**    It's time for us to part.

**Boy** (*plays a tune with the flute*)    My song will be heard all over the Colonus Forest. When you hear it, follow it to get out of the forest. With Oedipus. Do you promise?

**Old Poet**    Yes, I promise. With your song as a guide, we will get out of the forest together.

**Boy** (*stops on his way out*)    My name is Sophocles. I hate my father and my family name, but I hope you can still remember my name. So when you hear the song of Oedipus, and when Oedipus asks who the singer is, make sure to tell him. It's Sophocles of Colonus. Promise! Swear! (*Exits.*)

*Silence.*

*Sound of an owl.*

**Old Poet**    Huh huh – Now I'm really alone. The full moon is so bright it will never get dark . . . . . . So Dionysus' followers put on masks and transform? They reach a state of sharing his laughs and tears? Well, I have always wanted to reach such a state. (*Goes through his stuff and takes out a needle.*) What a sharp-looking needle. I've always been curious. Once the light is gone, what can you see in the dark? What could Oedipus rely on in a world devoid of light? . . . . . . Gods in charge of Colonus Forest, Poseidon's flying horse, I'm entering the darkness. Please reveal the path for me. (*Stabs his eyes with the needle.*)

*Neighing of Pegasus.*

*Darkness.*

*The forest reveals its path.*

*The full moon is bright.*


## Scene Fourteen: Once Upon a Time

*In this scene,* **Old Poet** *plays the role of* **Oedipus**.

*Under an ancient tree which no longer blooms,* **Oedipus**, *who is now old, is sitting with his back turned toward the audience. He is drinking.*

*Next to him, a crooked walking stick is leaning against the tree.*

**Antigone** *approaches* **Oedipus** (*played by* **Old Poet**).

**Antigone**    The people dwelling in the village. They probably enjoyed their dinner and are getting ready for bed. How warm the village lights must feel . . . Stop drinking. It's time to go to bed, Father.

**Oedipus**   The wind is wailing. Especially tonight.

**Antigone**   It's urging you to go to bed.

**Oedipus**   When you cannot see, your hearing becomes sharper. It's too dark here. Well, it's always dark for me. Antigone, I'm frightened. I'm living in the dark. That's why I drink. Without this, it feels even darker.

**Antigone**   You're a drunk.

**Oedipus** *laughs.*

**Antigone**   If you are that frightened, we can always go see people. Open the path to the forest. You know how to open it, right?

**Oedipus**   It's more frightening out there, with the people.

**Antigone**   But it's too lonely here. I miss people.

**Oedipus**   Do you think you'll feel less lonely with people around you? You have no idea. Feeling lonely among people is even more unbearable. So stop whining and try to sleep. Maybe you'll enjoy your dreams. Yes, dreams are sweet. In my dream, I am not blind. I can see just like I used to. I see your mother Jocasta and my young, vivacious friends.

**Antigone**   Don't just mumble things to yourself. It makes you look like a crazy old man, and that scares me . . . You're Oedipus. Pull yourself together and tell me about your proud old days. When you were young and spirited, when you beat the undefeated Sphinx.

**Oedipus**   Oh, that story. You didn't forget. Once upon a time. A long, long time ago, way before you were born, a creature called the Sphinx lived in Thebes. The Sphinx liked riddles, and she ate those who couldn't solve her riddles. One day I met this Sphinx creature. And she asked me a riddle.

**Antigone**   What walks on four legs upon birth and then later on two legs and then on three legs? What is that, father?

**Oedipus**   Human. A human like you. Newborn babies crawl on all fours. When they grow up, they walk on two legs.

**Antigone**   When they grow old like you, they walk on three, with a walking stick.

**Oedipus** (*laughs*)   Whose daughter is so smart? Here's another one who can beat the Sphinx. . . No, Antigone. Nothing is more dangerous than premature wisdom.

**Antigone**   There you go again. So what happened? Any more riddles?

**Oedipus**   . . . I forgot. That's all for the riddles. The drink must be working. My fingers and toes are getting warm. You should get some sleep. Just close your eyes tightly. Sleep visits only beneath eyelids. Who are you going to meet beneath your eyelids today? . . . . . . The last seed I planted, my last act of justice, did it fade without blooming? The corpses of those who died for our cause decomposed long ago. They must have become ant food and fox food, and now there's nothing left. Hope emptied of life. Corrupt futures . . . . . . Sleepy. I must go to bed. I'm not meeting anyone in my dreams . . . No humans . . . . . . (*Leans on the tree and falls asleep.*)

*Sound of flute.*

*The forest reveals its path.*

*Light comes in gradually.*

**Antigone** *stands up.*

**Antigone**    The forest—It can't be!—the forest is opening. . . . . . Father, the forest is revealing its path!

*Enter* **Boy** *with the flute, followed by* **Jocasta** *with flowers, and followers of* **Oedipus**.

*They offer flowers to* **Oedipus**.

*A bright light shines, and the* **Young Poet Boy** *recites.*

**Boy**
It's time to sing his finale.
He died lonely, yet
His death was not lonely.
The birds and trees sing his praise.
And people mourn his passing.
Justice will rise upon his death.
Someday when his song travels the world,
The dark Colonus Forest
Will open its path. Oh story,
Oh story, fly high, above, and yonder.

*Blackout.*

*End of play.*

## Notes

1    *Theogony*: a poem by Hesiod (8th–7th century BCE), written between 730 and 700 BCE, describing the origins and genealogies of the Greek Gods and how they gained control over the cosmos. What Tiresias recites is heavily truncated and edited.
2    Shakespeare, William. *Macbeth*, edited by Kenneth Muir, Methuen, 1971. 36–39 (Act I, Scene 7).
3    Shakespeare. *Macbeth*. 48–50 (Act II, Scene 1).
4    Sophocles, *Oedipus the King*. *Greek Tragedies I, 4th Edition*, edited and translated (into Korean) by Woohyun, Cho, Hyeonamsa, 1996, 195. The playwright writes: "This part is directly quoted from [a Korean translation of] Sophocles' *Oedipus the King* and gave me the inspiration for this play. Here I found the clue for updating the story."
5    Inscription on the column at the Temple of Apollo at Delphi. It means "do nothing in excess" (playwright's note).

# Sound of the Moon

## 달의 소리

A full-length historical drama

By Myung-Wha Kim
Translated from Korean into English by Walter Byongsok Chon
English Language Translation Consultant: Anne M. Hamilton

© 2026 by Byongsok Chon
All rights reserved

* The Korean production of *Sound of the Moon* premiered at Mary Hall in Sogang University as part of the 2006 Seoul Theater Festival, under the direction of Jung-Hee Park.

* This play has been translated with official permission from the author. The contract is available upon inquiry.

* The Daesan Foundation awarded a 2022 Grant for the Translation of Korean Literary Works to Walter Byongsok Chon and Anne Hamilton to create *An English Theatrical Translation of Korean Plays by Myung-Wha Kim*. This collection of four plays includes several genres exploring Korean history, culture, and sentiments, thereby enhancing intercultural theatrical exchange. Walter Byongsok Chon is the translator and Anne Hamilton is the English language translation consultant. The collection includes *Birds Don't Use a Crosswalk*, *Oedipus: The Fate of the Story*, *Sound of the Moon*, and *The Wind's Desire*.

* The translator and English language translation consultant were each awarded a Fellowship by the Bogliasco Foundation, and completed Spring 2024 Residencies in Bogliasco, Italy. *An English Theatrical Translation of Korean Plays by Myung-Wha Kim* was created with the support of a Bogliasco Foundation Fellowship.

# Characters

| | |
|---|---|
| **Yimoon** | *Male, young, Wooreuk's student.* |
| **Hyunduk** | *Male, young, Wooreuk's adopted son.* |
| **Gahkbi** | *Female, young, Wooreuk's adopted daughter.* |
| **Sangsa** | *Male, young, Wooreuk's student.* |
| **Princess** | *Female, young, Princess of Silla.*[1] |
| **Child Servant Yooldo** | *Male, young, the Princess' servant.* |
| **Wooreuk**[2] | *Male, elderly, the creator of the* gayageum.[3] |
| **Shaman** | *Female, any age.* |
| **The Spirit of Gahkbi's Mother** | *Female, middle-aged (If there is a need to double cast, the actress playing Gahkbi can also play this role.)* |
| **Voice, Servant** | *Offstage voices. Can be double cast.* |

# Time and Place

Mid-sixth century, the last year of King Beopheung of Silla.[4]
The stage represents the Gaya Confederacy[5] in peril and the Silla Kingdom emerging as a new empire.
Several trees are at the back of the stage.
The trees can be bamboo or aspen, with small leaves.

# Scenes

1. A Mountain
2. Wooreuk's House
3. A Dark and Empty Field
4. The Forest at Night
5. Wooreuk's House
6. The Palace
7. The Shaman's Forest
8. Wooreuk's House
9. The Palace
10. Gahkbi's Room
11. Near the Palace
12. The Princess' Chamber
13. Gahkbi's Rom
14. The Palace
15. Gahkbi's Yard

## History and Imagination

\* The playwright has created a period drama, portraying Wooreuk, the creator of the *gayageum*, an important traditional Korean stringed instrument; the Princess of Silla; and their musicians and families, in the context of changing sociological and political order. The historical record of this period is not complete and consistent. While Wooreuk and the Princess are historical figures, their actions and personal circumstances are imagined and given substance based on the playwright's research of Korean history.
\* This period drama is set in mid-sixth century Korea. The character Princess is the daughter of King Beopheung of Silla, the twenty-third monarch of Silla. The Princess is the kingdom's regent because her father has stepped away from his duties to live in a monastery. Her father was a member of the long-reigning Kim clan. Her mother, Queen Bodo, was a descendent of Pak Hyeokgeose, who was the founding monarch of Silla and the progenitor of the Park (*Pak, Bak*) clan. The Park clan is one of the most widespread clans in Korea, along with the Kim and Lee clans.

## Notes on the Text

\* The translation follows the original text's punctuation as much as possible in order to reflect the original language's pacing and the author's intention. The ellipses ". . . . . .", ". . .", and "–" appear in the Korean text.

> Note: In Western script notation, the playwright's use of ". . . . . ." can be interpreted as being similar to a (*Pause.*).
> Accordingly, ". . ." is similar to a (*Beat.*).
> And "–" is similar to a breath.

\* Notes provide explanations of specific Korean references for the reader's convenience.
\* This play contains songs. The lyrics appear in the script. For a production, new music needs to be composed for the songs.

## Content Warning

*This play contains physical violence and the depiction of mental breakdown.*

## Scene One

Setting: A Mountain.

*Traditional Korean music.*

**Hyunduk** *and* **Yimoon** *are looking down the mountain at the arrival of the* **Princess** *of Silla.*

**Yimoon**   That's something new. The way the sounds unite and split up is disorienting.

**Hyunduk**   That's what the common folk listens to nowadays.

**Yimoon**   The sound is sharp.

**Hyunduk**   It has iron in it.

**Yimoon**   Iron?

**Hyunduk**   I hear they melted iron to make musical instruments in the Qin Dynasty.[6] Perhaps that came in here.

**Yimoon**   The iron that's used for swords? For spears?

**Hyunduk**   Exactly. That ample sound, though, can be quite discomforting.

**Yimoon**   To see Silla making musical instruments out of iron.

**Hyunduk**   It's useless. The princess is deaf, so she can't hear anything. Look over there. That's the princess on the horse. I heard her mother poured poison in her ear when she was a child.

**Yimoon**   Her mother poured poison in her ear?

**Hyunduk**   That showed her power. It's fortunate she only lost her hearing, not her life. After that happened, the princess no longer laughed or cried. She's become more cruel and aggressive than her own father, King Beopheung.[7]

**Yimoon**   It's not handmade. That sound.

**Hyunduk**   Let's go.

**Yimoon**   It's coming from the windpipe. Some kind of a flute?

**Hyunduk**   Hey, Yimoon, that's trash. You'll hurt your ears.

**Yimoon**   But people love it.

**Hyunduk**   Father is waiting. We are late for practice.

**Yimoon**   Nobody listens to *our* music.

**Hyunduk**   Yimoon.

**Yimoon**   Master is drinking too much nowadays. He's getting more aggressive.

**Hyunduk**   After we lost our country, nothing matters to him anymore.

**Yimoon**    That's an excuse. He's your father, so of course you're defending him.

**Hyunduk**    Yimoon.

**Yimoon**    Hiding away like a bat, just because you lost your country? What did the country do for us, what did the corrupt King do for us? People are cunning. They change their family name and sneak into Silla so they can survive, and we're still idling around in the mountains. What's the point of our music when there's nobody to listen to it?

**Hyunduk**    Father is trying to preserve the music of Gaya. Somebody has to, with Silla seeking to wipe us out.

**Yimoon**    Music changes with the times. He's sticking with the old ways and always drinking. His mind is weak, and his skills are rusty. He can't even keep up with *me*. It's out of jealousy that he keeps beating me.

**Hyunduk**    That's not true. He's just lost.

**Yimoon**    The sound is gone! We missed it while chatting.

*He moves in order to hear the sound.*

**Hyunduk** (*stopping him*)    They'll see us. The princess is hot-tempered.

**Yimoon**    The princess likes music.

**Hyunduk**    She's deaf!

**Yimoon**    That's why she's traveling with musicians.

**Hyunduk**    She's traveling with them just in case. A lady shaman said that if the princess laughs or cries, she can rule the kingdom. That's why she travels with them. Listen closely. That's not music. It's the princess' desire that we're listening to.

**Yimoon**    The princess likes music. I hear she bestows gold to the musicians. Master used to play for the common folk. He also played for the King. He would boast that the black cranes in the palace flew down there to hear him play.

**Hyunduk**    We're from Gaya. I hear the Silla soldiers immediately kill the Gayans who are not naturalized.

**Yimoon**    Hyunduk. I want to see the world.

**Hyunduk**    Of course you do. (*Laughs.*) You haven't changed. Do you think seeing the world will ease this pain?

**Gahkbi** *enters, accompanied by* **Sangsa**.

**Gahkbi**    What's going on here?

**Hyunduk**    That's for me to ask. What's a grown woman like you doing all the way out here?

**Gahkbi**    I was picking spring greens. Father's not eating, just drinking. Yimoon, I picked some chrysanthemum. You like them pickled, right? Sangsa, bring the bucket. Look at these.

*Shows the bucket and starts singing.*

Spring is here
Spring greens are coming
Young and freshly plucked shepherd's purse
Wake up from your winter sleep
Harshly bitter chrysanthemum
Dry your eyes sweet daffodils
In full bloom all over the hills
Gather around –.

**Hyunduk**    Gahkbi is singing and dancing a lot these days. Her music is in full bloom.

**Gahkbi**    Blooming over here
Blooming over there –

**Gahkbi** *teasingly flirts with* **Yimoon**.

**Yimoon** *pushes away* **Sangsa** *and follows* **Gahkbi**.

**Yimoon**    Gahkbi. I'm craving meat, not greens.

**Gahkbi**    Uhmmm, what should I do? Shall I give you a piece of my thigh?

**Yimoon**    No, don't even joke about it. (**Gahkbi** *and* **Yimoon** *exit.*)
Blooming over here
Blooming over there –.

**Hyunduk** (*looks at them*)    She's just like her mother.

**Sangsa**    . . . . . .

**Hyunduk**    When Father first brought home Ghakbi and her mother, Gahkbi was tiny. She was skinny with sparkling eyes. When Father played music, she would just sit there by his side, with her eyes wide open.

**Sangsa**    She still has wide eyes.

**Hyunduk**    She's too much like her mother. The resemblance is uncanny.

**Sangsa**    Was her mother that elegant, too?

**Hyunduk** (*looks at him*)    Hey you, are you practicing enough?

**Sangsa**    Excuse me?

**Hyunduk**    If you lose your focus, you will fall behind. You haven't improved for months.

**Sangsa**    . . . . . .

**Hyunduk** (*while exiting with* **Sangsa**)    Chasing Gahkbi will not get you anywhere. She's been mastering music since she was five. (*They exit.*)

*Sound of birds.*

*Sound of the wind.*

*Birds' wings flutter.*

**Princess** (*offstage*)    Stop. I'll rest here.

**Child Servant** *enters with a stool, puts it down, and exits.*

**Princess** (*offstage*)    Where are we?

**Voice 1** (*offstage*)    We're in Gojami, from the old Garak Confederacy.[8]

**Princess** *enters, accompanied by* **Yooldo**.

**Princess**    The soil is fertile. Its soft and rich texture makes it optimal for growing grains. The surrounding mountains would have made it hard for father to conquer this land. We'll build a fort here and eliminate the last remnants of Gaya. (*Opens the document in her hand.*) What do you call this place again?

**Yooldo**    It's Gojami.

**Princess**    I asked what do you call this place?

**Yooldo**    It's Goja . . .

*As he makes eye contact with the* **Princess***, he remembers she is deaf.*

**Yooldo**    Oh, no, no!

**Princess**    Idiot. I said address me face to face.

**Yooldo**    I am beyond mortified, my princess. (*He rushes to face the* **Princess** *and moves along with her.*)

**Princess** (*thrashes* **Yooldo**)    Imbecile! Flea brain! Put your lips where my eyes can see. . . What do you call this place?

**Yooldo**    It's called Gojami.

**Princess** (*opens the document*)    Five ponies, a hundred sacks of millet, a hundred sacks of rice, and two slaves? Triple their offerings. No, make it five times. With this fertile soil, they can easily afford that much.

**Yooldo**    The princess says multiply their offerings by five.

**Voice 1** (*offstage*)    Multiply by five!

**Princess** (*touches her cheek*)    The wind is blowing. Yooldo, is the wind making any sound?

**Yooldo**    It is indeed. Each wind has its unique sound. This one is a breeze.

**Princess**    Unique sound? What sound is this place known for? Fertile soil must produce a beautiful sound.

**Yooldo**    I heard there is a musical instrument called *goh*.[9]

**Princess**    What kind of sound does it make? Does it make you laugh and cry?

**Yooldo**    I only heard it once. And the thing is, (*Waves his finger in the air.*) it makes a thin and light sound. You tie silk threads on a piece of wood, and you pluck the strings – *tung, tung* – like this. The soundboard creates a sound that resonates in the air.

*There is a sound of the* gayageum, *which makes* **Yooldo** *shake his body.*

*Tung*! Pure as a breeze. *Tung, tung*, like drops of water – the clear sound hits the ground and springs back up into the air. *Tung*!

*The sound of the* gayageum *becomes clearer, and* **Yooldo** *dances to it awkwardly.*

**Scene Two**

Setting: **Wooreuk**'s House.

*The sound of the* gayageum *continues.*

**Wooreuk** *is teaching his students.*

**Wooreuk**    Wrong. There's too much technique. The sound doesn't have a flow.

**Yimoon** *stops playing.*

**Wooreuk**    It's a vulgar sound you would hear in a brothel. What's gotten into you?

**Yimoon**    Last spring, out in the field, I came upon secular music.

**Wooreuk**    . . . . . .

**Yimoon**    It was so unique, I wanted to try it myself.

**Wooreuk**    Music should come from the heart, not out of imitation. Your heart is hopping all over the place. Keep it together.

**Gahkbi** (*laughs*)    Father, how do you keep a heart together? You can't even see the heart.

**Yimoon**    What can I do to keep it together?

**Wooreuk**    Let go of yourself. Your focus at the moment is solely on yourself.

**Gahkbi**    How do you let go of yourself? Like a rope? You're not making any sense –.

**Hyunduk**    Gahkbi, don't interrupt your father.

**Wooreuk**    Gahkbi, do you see that mountain? . . . How long has it been there? You see a mountain where there is a mountain, you see a tree where there is a tree. (**Gahkbi** *looks around slowly.*) The tree is swaying. What is making that tree sway? (**Gahkbi**, *closes her eyes.*) Embrace the swaying with your body.

**Gahkbi**    It's the lonesome breeze.[10]

**Gahkbi** *gets up and sings and dances to the wind.*

**Wooreuk**    Right it is. (*Gets up and dances, too.*)

**Hyunduk** *plays the* gayageum *to the dance.*

**Yimoon**    If you're supposed to play music from the heart rather than with your hands, what's the point of practicing? If the common folk's music is vulgar, then what is good music?

**Hyunduk**    Yimoon.

**Wooreuk**    Art is not about impressing people with skills.

**Yimoon**    If it is not about impressing people, then what is it about? You go through all this trouble just to play for the trees and the cranes? Isn't it selfish just to play for my own peace of mind? I want to play for the people.

**Gahkbi**    Father, let's stop here. I really need to pee.

**Yimoon**    You used to play for the people, master. You used to enjoy them cheering for you. I heard that you screamed on the street that you were the musician Wooreuk who won the favor of King Gasil of Gaya.[11] Also that you neglected your home for seven years, while you were trying to win the favor of the king, and that Gahkbi's mother found your neglect so unbearable that she finally killed herself.

**Wooreuk** *throws a piece of wood, which was next to him, strongly at* **Yimoon**. **Yimoon** *lets out a short scream and falls down.*

**Wooreuk**    I thought you were a rat with no integrity, but I raised a snake full of poison. How ungrateful.

**Yimoon** *gets up and leaves*

**Gahkbi**    Oh my, he's bleeding. What do we do?

**Gahkbi** *follows* **Yimoon**.

**Hyunduk**    I have no idea, either.

**Wooreuk**    . . . . . .

**Hyunduk**    What are we playing for?

**Wooreuk**    The sound itself.

**Hyunduk**    Then what am I? Why am I continuing on this uncertain path with no end in sight? Am I good enough to keep going?

**Wooreuk**    You think too much.

**Hyunduk**    We are all born with an innate unique quality. Yimoon hasn't been able to control his curiosity since he was a child. If he wanted to eat something, he would even go as far as stealing it to eat it. If he wanted to do something, he would not rest until he did it. That's who he is. That also earned him a lot of beatings. I was jealous of him at times. He would master something in a matter of months that would take me years to master. I wonder if I'm destined to end up just an ordinary musician as I'm not good enough to be your rightful successor.

**Wooreuk**   When all you do is think, you're never going to be good enough. (*Beats* **Hyunduk** *in anger.*) Stupid idiot.

**Hyunduk** (*taking the beating*)   I'm sorry, sir.

**Wooreuk**   When your fingers are moving, you don't need to think. There's ointment on the kitchen cabinet. Out.

**Hyunduk** *bows and exits.*

**Wooreuk**   When I first saw Yimoon, he was listening to the birds under a tree. He had been starving for days after his mother and father died in the commotion, and his eyes were blank. He had a stone in his hand to catch the birds, but he was so focused on the sound that he completely forgot his hunger.

**Sangsa**   Shall we take it from the top, master?

**Wooreuk**   I'm going to take a nap.

*He exits.*

**Sangsa** *is left alone.*

**Sangsa**   Master only listens to Yimoon playing. Gahkbi follows around Yimoon, and Hyunduk also cares only about Yimoon. I'm just a leftover. . . I practiced all night long, and yet I am only his shadow. (*He imitates* **Yimoon** *all of a sudden.*) What can I do to keep it together? If the common folk's music is vulgar, then what is good music?

*Blackout.*


**Scene Three**

Setting: A Dark and Empty Field.

*Dazzling* gayageum *sound.*

*Rough breathing of a man and woman.*

*The breathing softens.*

*Sound of the wind.*

**Yimoon** (*voice in the dark*)   Do you hear that?

**Gahkbi** (*voice in the dark*)   Hear what?

**Yimoon**   The wind.

**Gahkbi**   Oh.

*Sound of the wind.*

**Yimoon**   When I was a child, I feared that sound. On a winter night, the wind was howling through the doors. The wind was fierce the day we lost our country.

**Gahkbi**   The day we lost our country?

**Yimoon**   People were collapsing from cold and hunger, yet those who could kept going. The wind was so brutal, I thought it was going to snatch off my ears. Hum-hum.

**Gahkbi**   Shh!

**Yimoon**   What?

*Silence.*

*Sound of a baby wolf.*

*A faint silhouette of a man and woman.*

**Gahkbi**   It's a baby wolf. She sounds scared. Maybe she lost her mother.

**Yimoon**   You have good ears.

**Gahkbi**   Father taught me. (*Imitates her father.*) That sound is a baby wolf. That sound is a fox. That sound is the sound of hunger, and that is the sound of love. And that is the sound of fear.

**Yimoon**   Master taught you?

**Gahkbi**   But I don't know the sound of the heart yet.

**Yimoon** *and* **Gahkbi** *make love.*

*Intense sound of love making.*

*Intermittent sound of the wind.*

*Interspersed with the sounds of* **Yimoon** *and* **Gahkbi**.

*The two kinds of sounds may overlap.*

**Yimoon**   Tell me more about sounds. What sound do you hear now?

**Gahkbi**   Sound of the wind. The wind blowing through the willows . . . Sound of a beating heart . . . Sound of breathing. Your breath . . . Oh, it's hot! It's so hot it's killing me.

**Yimoon**   Gahkbi. Your sound is like a scream. Like metal. Tell me more, more, more, more!

**Gahkbi** *screams in ecstasy*

*Silence.*

*The moon shines brightly.*

*The two people who were in silhouette in the dark become visible.*

*There is also* **Sangsa** *who is on the lookout in one corner of the stage.*

**Yimoon** *puts on his clothes and his traveling attire.*

**Gahkbi**    So you're really leaving?

**Yimoon**    . . .

**Gahkbi**    When are you coming back?

**Yimoon**    . . .

**Gahkbi**    And your studies? You're not done yet.

**Yimoon**    Don't wait for me. I'm not coming back.

**Gahkbi**    . . . . . . It's cold.

**Yimoon** *puts his clothes on her*

**Gahkbi**    The moon is out.

**Yimoon** *looks at the moon*

**Gahkbi**    Father said if you listen with your heart, you can hear the sound of the moon.

**Yimoon**    The moon doesn't have a sound.

**Gahkbi**    That's not true. You know *Sa-mool*,[12] the *goh* piece that father composed. He said he was walking in the forest at night and suddenly heard the sound of the moon. At that moment, he felt that his mind went blank and that his body dissolved. He had the answer to life. He said the moon has a sound of rising and setting. And that the waves hear that sound. That's why there is the ebb and flow.

**Yimoon**    No way. He made that up.

**Gahkbi**    Jerk!

**Yimoon**    Gahkbi.

**Gahkbi**    Go, you bastard.

**Yimoon** (*stands up*)    Hey, Sangsa.

**Sangsa** *looks at* **Yimoon** *with intense hostility.*

**Yimoon**    Take her home. Master must be waiting.

*After* **Yimoon** *exits,* **Sangsa** *helps up* **Gahkbi**.

*When* **Gahkbi** *stumbles,* **Sangsa** *puts her on his back.*

*On one corner of the stage,* **Wooreuk** *is playing music.*

**Gahkbi** (*on* **Sangsa***'s back*)    Hey, Sangsa.

**Sangsa**    Yes.

**Gahkbi**    Do you hear that?

**Sangsa**    Hear what?

**Gahkbi**    The moon. The sound of the moon.

**Sangsa**    The moon?

**Gahkbi**    Yes. It's saying, "Hey, Gahkbi, where are you? Hey Sangsa, where are you?[13]

**Sangsa**    Oh, it's master. Yes, we're coming. (*They exit.*)

**Wooreuk**    Gahkbi, where are you? Sangsa, are you there? It's a full moon. I wish I had an audience today. . . The *goh* sounds the clearest on an autumn night. The moist sound from the summer monsoon turns heavy after the Full Moon Festival. I used to have an audience. She might have been sewing or sweeping the yard, but when she heard this piece, she would drop everything and run into my room. . . I couldn't finish the piece. That damn thing would just walk on air. And she's tormenting me, even now, after she has passed. See, Gahkbi, somebody used to like this sound. She was such a delicate creature and sensitive to sounds.

*When* **Wooreuk** *plays the* gayageum *again,*

**The Spirit of Gahkbi's Mother** *appears and sits in the back.*

*Sighing.*

**Wooreuk** *feels a chill all of a sudden, stops playing, and looks behind at* **The Spirit of Gahkbi's Mother**.

*The* **Spirit** *smiles.*

*The moon is bright.*

**Wooreuk** *resumes playing.*

*The* **Spirit** *rises and dances.*


**Scene Four**

Setting: The Forest at Night.

*The* **Shaman** *is holding a memorial service for those who lost their lives unjustly in the forest and now live there as vengeful spirits.*

**Yimoon** *appears with a bundle on his back.*

*The trees, surprised by this stranger, seem to cower and shiver.*

**Yimoon**    Who's there? Human or spirit?

**Shaman**    Am I human or spirit? I spend all my time with spirits, so now I'm not so sure anymore. I think I'm still human.

**Yimoon** (*sigh of relief*)    You almost gave me a heart attack.

**Shaman** (*laughs*)    You think spirits are scarier than humans?

**Yimoon**    Is this the shortcut to the palace in Seorabeol?[14]

**Shaman**   Young man. How reckless of you to come to this part of the forest this late at night. This forest is the home of the vengeful spirits of Goryeong Gaya.[15] The last battle between Silla and Goryeong Gaya took place right here. (*Remote screams.*) Thousands died here. The forest is over-occupied with vengeful spirits, so people don't even come near here during the day. What business does a tenderfoot like yourself have coming through here?

**Yimoon**   For God's sake, how do I get out of here?

**Shaman**   I'll tell you for a piece of iron.[16]

**Yimoon**   There.

**Shaman**   Goody. Since Silla took our country, you can't do anything without iron. A ghost would come running for it. Oh, there's another one.

**Yimoon**   Where, where?

**Shaman** (*laughs*)   Scared you, didn't I? Do you think ghosts only live in the forest and not around you? Your dead parents are sitting right on your shoulders. Right? Your parents are dead, right?

**Yimoon**   Multitudes died in the war. Stop this nonsense and tell me how to get to the Seorabeol Palace.

**Shaman**   You can enter the forest of your own free will, but leaving is a different matter. Give me another piece. Then I'll show you the way and also exorcise the evil spirit that's stuck on you. I have a song for every kind of exorcism.

**Yimoon**   I already gave you one.

**Shaman**   That's not enough. The ghosts need a real offering.

**Yimoon** (*suddenly chokes the* **Shaman**)   Tell me how I can get to the Seorabeol Palace.

**Shaman**   Help! You should be afraid of who I really am. Please let me live. It's over there, that way.

**Yimoon**   You should have done that to begin with. (*Exits.*)

**Shaman** *falls down to the ground and starts singing*
    Hovering all over the streets
    Spirit of protection
    Spirit of fire and ashes
    Spirit of parting
    Spirit in mourning of her parents
    Spirit of cloth hiding under the shelf
    Spirit moving from wall to wall.[17] . . .

Cursed one, ill fate awaits you on your path. You'll go blind, deaf, and hungry. (*Sings.*)
    Spirit of the mountain
    Spirit of the tree in the forest
    Oak tree, cassia tree

Mulberry tree, zelkova tree
Kalopanax–[18]
Kalo kalo kalo panax
Prickly kalopanax
Spirits who died unjustly in the war
Descend. Wooh—.

*The trees dance.*

*The spirits descend among the trees.*

*The spirits and the trees dance together.*

**Scene Five**

Setting: **Wooreuk**'s House.

**Gahkbi** *packs up the bundle for* **Sangsa**.

**Hyunduk** *tries to stop her.*

**Hyunduk**    What's the point?

**Gahkbi**    This is raw rice. If you run out of food, help yourself to this. I also packed some socks. I actually made these for Yimoon, and they might be too big for you. But take them to keep your feet warm. I put extra rabbit fur inside this jacket. I got it for father last winter, but now it's yours. For Father, I can heat up the room.

**Hyunduk**    Gahkbi.

**Gahkbi**    This is a gold ring. It was my mother's. If you run out of money, sell this.

**Hyunduk**    Sangsa has just learned the basic technique. He can't miss his lessons.

**Gahkbi**    I really need Yimoon now. I hate to give birth without the baby's father. Sangsa, you're my only hope. Bring him home. If you do, you can have anything you want.

**Hyunduk**    It's a big world. How is he supposed to find Yimoon?

**Gahkbi** (*to* **Sangsa**)    You like me, right? When you bring Yimoon, I will let you touch me. I know you've been leering at me. I could feel it in the back of my head. Your eyes were always burning with desire.

**Hyunduk**    You hopeless fool. Then why did you let Yimoon go in the first place?

**Gahkbi**    How could I have known that he would really leave? I thought he would be back in about ten days. Even if he wasn't, I never expected it to feel like my heart is getting ripped out. It's like my liver is turning inside out.

**Sangsa**    I'll bring him home.

**Hyunduk** (*to* **Sangsa**)    Nonsense. You must realize the importance of this stage in your practice. If you stop now, everything you've worked for will be gone.

**Sangsa**    People come first.

*He picks up the bundle and leaves.*

*Sound of wind.*

**Hyunduk**    It will be easier to catch the wind. Since Yimoon left of his own free will, do you really think you can change his mind?

**Gahkbi**    I am pregnant. I will have him back. Even if he is way up in the sky or deep down in the sea. (*Quick exhale.*) Hyunduk. The baby's kicking.

**Hyunduk**    . . . . . .

**Gahkbi** (*to her baby, putting* **Hyunduk**'*s hand on her stomach*)    This is your uncle. His fingers are callused. It's because he practices every day. Once you are born, you will learn music from him. (*Laughs, to* **Hyunduk**.) Its strength is astounding. Listen, brother. There's a life breathing inside of me. It has Yimoon's strength.

**Hyunduk** *looks blankly.*

*Dum dum dum sound, like a baby kicking, like a drum.*


**Scene Six**

Setting: The Palace.

**Yimoon** *and* **Yooldo** *play the drums and enter to the drumbeat.*

**Yooldo** *is already drunk.*

**Yooldo**    Damn, am I drunk already? Your beat is all wrong. It sounds so much more complicated than what I just taught you. Listen carefully. (*Plays a simple beat.*)

**Yimoon** *copies him exactly.*

**Yooldo**    You got that at once. With your skill, you can have a bright future here. You know how much our princess adores musicians. A famous shaman once said, when the princess laughs and cries, she will ascend the throne. The thing is, only music makes her laugh and cry. Funny, right? Since she's deaf. And here we are, musicians making and playing music. That's why she's enamored of us. (*Plays the drum.*)

**Yimoon** *repeats the beat*

**Yooldo**    Look at you!

*He repeats it and adds to it.*

**Yimoon** *repeats it and adds to it*

*They play music for a while.*

*Enter the* **Princess**.

**Princess**    Who's this? . . . I haven't seen him before.

**Yooldo**    He's a new musician.

**Princess**    What's your name?

**Yimoon** (*with his head down, too afraid to look at her directly*)    It's Yimoon.

**Princess**    I asked you what your name was.

**Yimoon**    It's Yimoon.

**Princess**    Are you stupid? Tell me your name right now.

**Yooldo**    She's deaf. Show her your lips.

**Yimoon** (*looks at her*)    It's Yimoon.

**Princess**    Assist Yooldo.

*The* **Princess** *sits, and* **Yooldo** *opens the box of musical instruments.*

**Princess**    What's the tune for today?

**Yooldo** *takes out the flute and plays it immediately.*

**Princess**    I see nothing special. You think that will make me laugh and cry? Next.

**Yooldo** (*takes out* yo)    This is called *yo*, and it's an iron drum.

**Princess**    Iron that makes spears and swords?

**Yooldo**    Yes. It's a valuable import from the Qin Dynasty.

**Princess**    What kind of a sound can that tiny thing make?

**Yooldo** *plays it.*

**Princess**    Oh! The air feels different. The iron is strong. Do swords make this kind of sound on the battlefield?

**Yooldo**    The same iron can make different sounds.

**Princess**    Different?

**Yooldo**    Depending on their function. The function of a musical instrument is to create a sound pleasing to the ear, so the sound is harmonious, buoyant, and clear. The function of a sword is to kill, so the sound is cold and sharp. The sword sound is so heavy and low for an ordinary person to perceive, but a war veteran can hear a sword cry.

**Princess**    What kinds of cries are in this world?

**Yooldo**    The world was born with a cry. Every birth begins with a cry. You were born with a cry, too. You held your fists tight like this, *waw waw*, not wanting to be born, *waw waw*.

**Princess**    People have tears when they cry. Why don't you have tears?

**Yooldo**    You are correct. I was only pretending, but people do have tears when they cry. To cry, people must feel sad.

**Princess**    Feel sad?

**Yooldo**   Feeling sad is, how shall I put it, feeling hurt and deprived and hopeless, in spite of oneself.

**Princess**   Like anger?

**Yooldo**   Anger is a destructive force and is different from feeling sad and crying. Sadness comes from feeling cleansed, tender, regretful, and mistreated. It evokes pity and benevolence. Yes, sadness evokes benevolence!

**Princess**   You said that every birth begins with a cry.

**Yooldo**   Yes, it does.

**Princess**   Does every being then feel all those emotions?

**Yooldo**   Certainly. A bird feels sad and cries, and a mosquito cries because each day is a struggle. The wind cries because it can't stop blowing, and the river cries because it can't stop flowing. A child cries, and a dog cries, and everyone cries.

**Princess**   . . . . . . Does the moon up there cry, too?

**Yooldo**   The moon? I'm not sure. Is rain just the moon's tears? I'm afraid I have not heard anything about the moon crying.

**Yimoon**   I heard that the moon makes a sound.

**Yooldo**   Hey. How dare you?

**Princess** (*looks at* **Yimoon**)   What did you just say?

**Yimoon**   I heard that when you listen with your heart, you can hear the sound of the moon. The darkness of my heart kept me from hearing the moon, but I did hear that the moon has a sound. So, I'm sure the moon cries, too.

**Princess**   How can you be sure when you have not heard it yourself?

**Yimoon**   I heard that a musician from Gaya heard the sound of the moon and composed a piece called *Sa-mool*.

**Princess**   What's the name of that musician?

**Yimoon**   His name is Wooreuk.

**Princess**   How do you know a musician from Gaya?

**Yimoon**   . . . . . . His fame reached my ears.

**Princess**   Yooldo.

**Yooldo**   Yes, princess.

**Princess**   Capture the sound of the moon.

**Yooldo**   I'm sorry?

**Princess**   Bring me the Gayan musician who composed the sound of the moon. Gather every cry in this world and all the sounds I have not heard, put them together in a sack, and present them to me. (*To* **Yimoon**.) What did you say your name was?

**Yimoon**    It's Yimoon.

**Princess**    What a pretty face. Follow me.

*The* **Princess** *and* **Yimoon** *exit.*

**Yooldo**    What on earth is happening? She demands the sound of the moon, and if I say it's impossible, I'll surely get in trouble. Then should I travel to the moon? The moon. How do I get there? Should I ask the man in the moon? Would he understand me? What about the musician from Gaya? I heard our soldiers are killing every Gayan they spot, so would there even be any survivors? My heavens! (*Kicks off his shoe.*)[19] That way.

*He goes in the direction of his shoe.*


**Scene Seven**

Setting: The **Shaman**'s Forest.

**Sangsa** *arrives at the Shaman's Forest.*

*The* **Shaman** *is in the middle of an exorcism.*

**Sangsa** (*to the* **Shaman**)    Have you seen anyone passing through here?

**Shaman**    Ghost or human?

**Sangsa**    Either.

**Shaman**    Ghosts, plenty; human, there was one.

**Sangsa**    Was he young? Where did he go?

**Shaman**    I'll tell you for some iron.

**Sangsa** *gives her a piece of iron.*

**Shaman**    Just one piece? Hold on. The ghosts are descending to the earth. *Woo—*

*Sings a nonsensical song.*

Here comes the ghost from the east. *Woo—*

*The leaves are shaking.*

**Yooldo** *arrives at the forest.*

**Yooldo**    Greetings, madam. I am Yooldo, a musician from the Seorabeol Palace. I'm the master musician. The princess is gathering the sounds from the world, and this damn rookie showed up and – oh, there are two of you here. Which of you is the last Shaman of Gaya? Anyway, the shaman, I mean the princess said, now where was I? Right, this young musician mentioned that there is a musician called Wooreuk who plays the sound of the moon, and the princess ordered me to capture the sound of the moon –

**Sangsa** *jumps on* **Yooldo** *and grabs him by the collar.*

**Shaman**    Spirits, descend!

*The spirits descend.*

**Sangsa**    Did you just say Wooreuk?

**Yooldo**    I was too disoriented to remember exactly what I said.

**Sangsa**    And you are from the Seorabeol Palace?

**Yooldo** (*taken by surprise*)    Yes, sir. The Seorabeol Palace it is. Oh, I remember, I said this young man mentioned that there is a musician called Wooreuk who plays the sound of the moon! I did say Wooreuk.

*Upon hearing this,* **The Spirit of Gahkbi's Mother** *climbs onto* **Yooldo**'s *back.*

**Yooldo**    Why do I feel so heavy all of a sudden? So, anyway dearly respected shaman, Yimoon or Yisun or whatever blabs about this conman musician playing the sound of the moon, and the princess, who is deaf by the way, cannot tell that it's a lie. So, she orders me to capture the sound of the moon.

**Sangsa**    Princess?

**Yooldo**    Yes, the Princess of Seorabeol.

**Sangsa** *exits, running in the direction of the palace.*

**Yooldo**    Dear shaman, where are you going?[20] I walked for days to get to you, shaman!

**Shaman**    Why do you keep shouting? You're disrupting my concentration. I'm not going anywhere. I'm right here.

**Yooldo**    You're a shaman, too?

**Shaman**    Isn't that what *you*'ve been calling me? What's this about again?

**Yooldo**    The sound of the moon.

**Shaman**    Right, you asked if anyone passed through here. There was a young man. Now when was that?

**Yooldo** (*pointing in the direction that* **Sangsa** *exited*)    Just now.

**Shaman**    About ten months ago. He was heading to the Seorabeol Palace.

**Yooldo**    I just came from the Seorabeol Palace.

**Shaman**    Words keep spinning round and round, and that means something ominous dwells in the air. Today is the day that Gaya perished, so the ghosts are emitting sinister energies. You're talking nonsense, so something must be weighing you down. Give me another piece of iron. There's a ghost on your back. That's why you feel heavy. I'll set her free.

**Yooldo** (*gives her a piece of iron*)    You're correct, I do feel heavy. But, dear shaman, there's no time to play with ghosts now, I have to catch the sound of the moon.

**Shaman** (*sings*)
> Come on over here
> Sad or angry
> May you feel as you feel
> Let me feed you if you are hungry
> Let me clothe you if you're cold
> May you forget all you regret.

*Hums.*
> – – – Return, ghost from the east.

**Yooldo**    What's wrong with this Gayan forest? There are ghosts everywhere. Come ghosts or humans, I've made it this far. Come to think of it, these are all some kinds of sounds. (*Opens the sack he brought and gathers the sounds.*) The shaman is making a sound under the moon, so that makes it the sound of the moon. (*Imitates the* **Shaman.**)

> *Woo* – – – – return, ghost from the east.

*The trees shake.*

*Sound of the wind.*

**The Spirit of Gahkbi's Mother** *smiles at the moon.*


**Scene Eight**

Setting: **Wooreuk**'s House.

**Wooreuk** *is tuning the* gayageum *strings.*

**Wooreuk**    I admit, I hadn't been home much. I couldn't find a peace of mind. The fate of the country was hanging by a thread, and the pursuit of sound was an endless, hopeless ordeal. She was capricious. Still I wouldn't dream of bringing in another man to a home with children. A real mother wouldn't do that kind of thing. . . If she was going to hang herself, she could have at least done it far away, instead of right here.

*He feels chills and looks back.*

**The Spirit of Gahkbi's Mother** *is right there.*

**Wooreuk**    Cruel one. What unfinished business can you still have left here to torment me even as a spirit? Out.

**Hyunduk** *enters with a baby wrapped in a baby quilt and sits down.*

**Hyunduk**    Father, I have to tell you something.

**Wooreuk**    . . . . . . Hyunduk. I've been seeing things recently.

**Hyunduk**    You've gotten weak.

**Wooreuk**    My time is near.

**Hyunduk**    It's my fault. With us having only sprouts to eat.

**Wooreuk**    Any news about Yimoon?

**Hyunduk**    Sangsa will bring him back soon.

**Wooreuk**    I heard they kill any Gojami nobles they find down the mountain.

**Hyunduk**    He's smart, so he can take care of himself.

**Wooreuk**    Is this it? The tradition of Gayan music is not set in place yet. My successor took off. With Yimoon out of the picture, my new successor is you, Hyunduk. Gahkbi hasn't been around at all recently. I guess she gave up on the study of sound.

**Hyunduk** (*puts the baby in the quilt in front of* **Wooreuk**)    This is Gahkbi's child.

**Wooreuk**    . . . . . . Who's the father?

**Hyunduk**    It's Yimoon.

**Wooreuk**    Like mother, like daughter. After the three-week period of maternal care, throw out both the mother and the baby.

**Hyunduk**    That might literally kill Gahkbi. With her temper, abandonment might lead her to desperate measures. And he is just a new-born.

**Wooreuk**    . . . . . .

**Hyunduk**    She gave birth without the father. Please don't abandon them. (*Gets down on his knees.*)

**Wooreuk**    Throw them out.

*He plays the* gayageum.

*His playing overlaps with the baby crying.*

**Hyunduk**    Even animals protect their offspring, so how can you, as a father, kill your own child? Does the pursuit of music require that kind of cruelty? People come first. What's the use of the law, what's the use of justice, if it doesn't concern people? If only you hadn't thrown out Gahkbi's mother back then.

**Wooreuk**    How dare you –!

*He beats up* **Hyunduk**, *and* **Hyunduk** *does not resist.*

**Hyunduk**    Father! For the first time in my life, I'm disobeying you. Please let me, just once. Gahkbi is my sister. Yes, she's my stepsister, but she's so caring she could be my real sister. She ended up that way because she is naïve and kind, not because she is a shrew. She's the only bloodline of her mother. And her mother was like a real mother to me. I was too young to stop you back then, but not this time. If I can't protect Gahkbi, how can I face her mother? Father, please –.

**Wooreuk**    Gahkbi is a useless instrument with broken strings. Her blood was tainted to begin with.

*Baby cries.*

**Wooreuk** (*sighs*)    Take care of them. You make the decisions now, not me. (*Exits.*)

**Hyunduk** (*rushes after him in case* **Wooreuk** *might change his mind*)    Thank you, father. Thank you. Gahkbi, hey Gahkbi!

**The Spirit of Gahkbi's Mother** *picks up the baby and comforts him.*

**The Spirit of Gahkbi's Mother** (*sings*)

    Hush little baby, sweet little baby
    Don't you cry, just dream away
    Delay the morning call, little cock
    Let our baby sleep safe and sound
    Dear golden child, dear silver child.

*Blackout.*


**Scene Nine**

Setting: The Palace.

*The* **Princess** *runs in, laughing.*

**Yimoon** *and* **Yooldo** *run after her.*

**Yooldo** *is holding the sack full of sounds and waits for a chance to tell the* **Princess**.

**Princess**    *Hahahahahaha –.*

**Yimoon**    If you nod your head from time to time, you will look more dignified.

**Princess** (*nods her head after him*)    *Hahahahahaha –.*

**Yooldo** (*opens the sack*)    Princess, look at all the sounds in –.

**Princess**    My mouth hurts. Do I have to open it this wide?

**Yimoon**    This is a general's laughter.

**Princess**    What other kinds are there?

**Yimoon**    There are some where you open your mouth just a little bit. Maidens and ladies have that laugh.

**Princess**    That might hurt less. Show me.

**Yimoon**    You cover your mouth with your hand like this, and then *hohohohohoho. Hohohohohoho.*

**Princess** (*repeats*)    *Hohohohohoho.*

**Yimoon**    It's better if you can twist your waist a little bit.

**Princess** (*repeats*)    *Hohohohohohoho –.* Why do people laugh like this?

**Yimoon**   Because they feel.

**Princess**   Feel?

**Yimoon**   When you feel excited, your lungs tingle and get wrinkled. Those wrinkles make you laugh. You laugh when you feel something is fun, thrilling, satisfying, or silly.

**Princess**   Feel something? Then my lougher without feeling must be empty.

*Suddenly feels melancholy*

Yooldo. What sounds did you bring?

**Yooldo**   Princess, I put all kinds of sounds in this sack. (*Goes through the sack.*)

This is the wind howling. You can hear it in the bamboo grove on a gloomy autumn day. *Wheeeee* — This is an angry thunder. It wails, convulsing its shoulders. There is also an ear-piercing ghost howl, as well as sounds of summoning the ghost and casting out the ghost.

**Princess**   A sound summoning the ghost? Well, far north in the Nakrang Kingdom,[21] I hear there is a peculiar drum that automatically beats when there is an invasion. That drumbeat rumbles through the whole kingdom and crushes the enemy.

**Yimoon**   The Drum of Nakrang?

**Princess**   Father once told me of even more peculiar sounds recorded in *The Book of Sounds* from the Qin Dynasty. The sound of falling rain, the sound of the earth splitting open. Sounds are enigmatic.

**Yooldo**   *Whoooh – – – – – – – –*

*Sings and dances.*

> God of the east sea in the east
> God of the underworld in the west
> God of the south sea in the south
> God of the burial in the north
> North, south, east, west
> All around us in all directions
> High and low, far and close.
> *Whoooh – – whoooh – –.*

**Princess**   Stop it! That's painful. When you sing that song, you're basically inviting ghosts to the palace. I don't want to encounter the ghosts of those who were tortured and died in the war. All I am interested in now is the sound of laughter.

**Yooldo** (*aside*)   Damn it. Didn't she ask for the sound of suffering? How am I supposed to present the sound of laughter all of a sudden? (*Pretends to go through the sack. To the* **Princess**) Yes, princess. I found the sound of laughter. This is a dog laughing.

**Princess**   Does a dog laugh?

**Yooldo**   Indeed, princess. Absurd things make a stray dog laugh.[22]

**Princess**   Laugh like a dog.

**Yooldo**   *Bow – Wow –*. The world is such a mess *Bow – Wow –* All I can do is bark like a dog. *Bow – Wow –*

**Princess**   Last time you said a dog cries. Now cry like a dog.

**Yooldo** (*same sound*)   *Bow – Wow –*. *Bow – Wow –*

**Princess**   Your mouth looks exactly the same. Are you sure you brought the correct sounds? I told you to bring me the sound of the moon. Let me hear it.

**Yooldo** (*as a last resort, he takes out a musical instrument from the sack*)   Certainly, princess. This is the Gayan instrument called *goh*, which makes the sound of the moon.

**Princess**   Is that so? Then play me the sound of the moon.

**Yooldo**   The sound of the moon? I'm not from Gaya. So the thing with this instrument is that it plays itself when the moon rises, and stops when the moon sets. Dear princess, I haven't really learned how to play it. I have committed a mortal sin.

**Yimoon**   Princess, I can't play the sound of the moon, but I can play that instrument.

**Yimoon** *takes the* goh *and starts playing.*

*The* **Princess** *watches.*

**Princess**   Your fingers fly like a butterfly. You're not just a handsome face, you've also got skills. You are my new favorite. Yooldo. You didn't bring me the sound of the moon. Instead, you sang the ghost song and deeply offended me. Yimoon will take your place from now on. You will take thirty swats with the paddle and are demoted to Yimoon's servant. (*Picks up the paddle and tries to catch* **Yooldo**.) Scoundrel, get back here. Right now.

**Yooldo** (*running away*)   Please spare my life, dear princess. Have mercy. I beg you.

**Yimoon** (*laughs out loud*)   Princess, *this* is laughter. You laugh like this when you see an old friend. (*To the* goh) *Goh* from Gaya. It's good to see you again, my friend. You've been an enormous help today. My precious and invaluable friend.

*He laughs out loud again.* **Yooldo** *runs by him.*

**Yimoon**   Scoundrel, get back here. *Hahahahha –.*

*He picks up the* goh *and follows him.*


**Scene Ten**

Setting: **Gahkbi**'s Room.

**Gahkbi** *has a liquor bottle in front of her.*

**Gahkbi**   I can't see a thing.

**Hyunduk**   You're drinking again. You'll catch a cold, leaving the windows wide open like this in the winter.

**Gahkbi**   The snow covered the whole world. The night covered the whole snow. It was all white, now it's all dark.

**Hyunduk**   We have a deer in the barn. You know, the wild animals come down to the village because they have nothing to eat. This deer, maybe he sprained his foot or something, he can't walk right and doesn't even run away when he sees people. I guess he must be exhausted, too, with nothing to eat. Where's Chanwoo? He may like to see the deer.

**Gahkbi**   . . . . . .

**Hyunduk**   Hey, Gahkbi.

**Gahkbi**   In the west, I heard there's a liquor called the drink of forgetfulness. You drink that, and you forget everything. I wish I could have a sip.

**Hyunduk**   You'd better not. It's so strong you will have no memory left. You'll forget your parents, your siblings, your house, and everything else. You'll even forget all the singing and dancing and playing the *goh* for over ten years.

**Gahkbi**   To hell with all that. I wish I could forget it all.

**Hyunduk**   You'll also forget Chanwoo.

**Gahkbi**   Chanwoo? No. I'm not forgetting Chanwoo.

**Hyunduk**   Yeah. A mother shouldn't. It's time you get yourself together and start practicing again.

**Gahkbi**   The *goh* that father plays is a fake. There's no sadness. How can he make such beautiful and carefree sound after killing mom? It's all fake. I'm not doing that anymore.

**Hyunduk**   Stop drinking.

**Gahkbi**   My fingers are soft again. The calluses are gone. I *will* forget the *goh* and everything, even without the western drink. But brother, how come I can't forget him?

**Hyunduk**   . . . . . .

**Gahkbi**   Do you think Mom was in so much pain as well? I can't remember much.

**Hyunduk**   Your mother had milky skin. When I first saw her, I was captivated by her powder smell. A warm spring day always brings back the memory of her smell. Wherever she went, she brought warmth. She smiled a lot. Even when I was naughty, she always gave me a smile.

**Gahkbi**   My only memory of her is her crying. Even on the day before she hung herself, she cried alone. She smiled when she saw me, but her eyes were teary. Mom, don't cry, don't cry, Mom. It was strange. How she could cry and smile at the same time.

**Hyunduk**   She was so delicate she couldn't stand loneliness. But who can? Look at that deer. No living creature, no matter what kind, can stand loneliness and hunger.

**Gahkbi**   When father would play back in the day, the world stood still, and a crane danced to the tunes. The King embraced father with both arms. When the whole world was crazy about him, Mom was dying. He abandoned Mom just so that he could play for the corrupt King. He couldn't even hear Mom's pain because he was too busy cheering up that drunk. That King ruined our country, yes he did.

**Hyunduk**   I'm sure Father was in pain, too.

**Gahkbi** (*drunk*)   That, is the essence of sound.

**Hyunduk**   Gahkbi.

**Gahkbi**   Brother, look how time just passes. And I'm breaking down.

*She is drunk and lies on the floor.*

**Hyunduk** *takes off his shirt and covers her with it.*

*He picks up the liquor bottle and drinks from it himself.*

**Scene Eleven**

Setting: Near the Palace.

**Sangsa**   So tall, so huge, this Silla palace. Not even an eagle can fly that high. They're guarding the palace like a fortress. Not even an ant can go through security here. Yimoon, are you in there? Bastard! He must be cozy in a heated room. While I was chewing raw rice, he must have enjoyed meat and fully cooked rice. While I had to curl up trying to sleep on a cold floor, he must have covered himself with a silk blanket. I'm not cold. Gahkbi gave me this rabbit coat and also these socks which she made especially for you. My feet are burning with jealousy. I'm coming for you, Yimoon.

**Yooldo** *enters carefully.*

**Yooldo**   *Whoo Whoo.*

**Sangsa**   *Whoo Whoo.*

**Yooldo**   You almost gave me a heart attack.

**Sangsa**   And the stuff?

**Yooldo**   Show me first.

**Sangsa**   You sure you have everything?

**Yooldo**   You bet. I lived in the palace as the princess' music teacher for ten years. I would have been appointed as chief music master, if only that thief Yimoon or Yisun hadn't shown up a few years ago. I'm telling you.

**Sangsa** (*throwing him the bundle that* **Gahkbi** *packed*)    Here's the rice and iron.

**Yooldo**    You also promised me a gold ring.

**Sangsa**    Alright, there. (*Gives him the gold ring.*) Now it's your turn.

**Yooldo**    It's all in this map right here. There are three paths. Underground. Beneath the pond. And the back door. Over there is the secret passage leading to the backdoor. Only a few long-term loyal subjects know about the secret passage.

**Sangsa**    And the powder?

**Yooldo**    Here. It's a specialty from the Qin Dynasty. Half of it will make the heart swell, and all of it will blow it up. So use it with discretion.

*He giggles.*

**Sangsa**    What does this Yimoon teach the princess?

**Yooldo**    He teaches sound to a deaf person. Like how to play the Gayan musical instrument. Come to think of it, that's bizarre. He claims he's from Silla, so how come he can play a Gayan instrument? Since we're killing all the Gayans, maybe he pretended to be from Silla and snuck into the palace. (*Catches* **Sangsa** *who was about to leave.*) Young man, if you get caught, we've never met.

**Sangsa**    Sure.

*He exits.*

**Yooldo** (*growing sound of wind and wolves*)    The wind is fierce. Such a dark and dreary day, it's perfect for revenge. What's next for me? Dear wind, what's in store for this lone wolf who turned his back on this world? (*Throws one of his shoes.*) That way. . . Really, what do I do now? Since I learned how to exorcise ghosts, maybe I can do that.

*Sings:*

> From the east comes god of the east sea
> Looking down from the west
> Is god of the underworld.
> *Whoo whoo – –.*

*The trees dance.*


**Scene Twelve**

Setting: The **Princess'** Chamber.

*The* **Princess** *and* **Yimoon** *are asleep. The* **Princess** *wakes up screaming.*

**Yimoon**    Princess, are you alright?

*Holds her by the arms.*

**Princess**   Who's this? . . . Oh, it's you, Yimoon. I can't see your lips. Come closer.

**Yimoon**   Are you alright?

**Princess** (*touches* **Yimoon**'s *face and holds him close*)   I had a dream. Someone entered this chamber. I was too frightened to make any sound. All I could do was hide under the blanket. I should have checked who the intruder was, but I just couldn't.

**Yimoon**   It's alright now.

*Moonlight shines in.*

**Princess**   The moon lights up the room. I can see your face now.

**Yimoon**   You're drenched in sweat.

**Princess**   I was, even in my dream. It's like I have a well inside me. Even my dry tongue feels moist. Last night, deep inside, my body felt wet. Yimoon, is this what causes crying?

**Yimoon**   It is, indeed.

**Princess**   Lick my sweat.

**Yimoon** *licks her sweat.*

**Princess**   How is it?

**Yimoon**   Salty.

**Princess**   Are tears also salty?

**Yimoon**   Yes, salty and unpleasant.

**Princess**   I thought tears were sweet. So they're salty. . . . . . My mother, Queen Bodo,[23] was a descendant of Pak Hyeokgeose.[24] King Michu[25] was the first king in the Kim clan in Silla, and later King Naemul[26] continued the Kim clan's reign over Silla. The Kim clan and the Pak clan hated each other despite our bonds. My mother was beautiful and fierce. My father's coldness and contempt could not shake her. On starry nights, she would lay me on her lap and clean my ears. That's what I expected that night, too. I wondered why she would clean my ears when I was already asleep. That's the question I kept asking, in between dreams, even when she was pouring poison in my ears.

**Yimoon**   That's beyond shocking.

**Princess**   She must have thought, without me, Father wouldn't have anyone to succeed him, and then the Pak clan could take the throne again. That's atrocious. Even after everything I've been through, my senile father still wouldn't let me take the throne. Even after my husband was poisoned to death, Father could not stand up to the high officials who were trying to reestablish the reign of the Pak clan. All he did was take another wife, a young one. If she gives birth to a son, who do I have left on my side in this palace? How many more enemies will I have in Silla?

**Yimoon**    The mighty have no enemies. Might rules the world. Become the mighty. You'll have no enemies, only followers. A mighty princess, that is who you are. Silla is stronger and richer under your interim reign now, more so than under your father King Beopheung's.[27]

**Princess**    Your prose feels like silk. You have a gift for comforting.

**Yimoon**    Your compliment is an immense honor.

**Princess**    I want to give you a present. What do you desire?

**Yimoon**    Nothing except your presence and the study of sound. But if I might ask for one thing.

**Princess**    One thing?

**Yimoon**    It is *The Book of Sounds* from the Qin Dynasty.

**Princess**    That's confidential! How dare you?

**Yimoon** (*gets on his knees and bows down*)    Please forgive my impudence.

**Princess** (*gets him up and examines him closely*)    The moonlight highlights the splendor of your body. Look at those muscles. Yimoon, tell me more about the body's waters. Tears. Sweat and spit. And semen. What else is there?

**Yimoon**    There's blood.

**Princess**    They're all warm.

**Yimoon**    And pee.

**Princess** (*laughs*)    What does pee sound like?

**Yimoon**    *Sheeeeee – – – – – –*

**Princess** (*she copies him and suddenly stops.*)    Yimoon, did I just laugh?

**Yimoon**    Sorry?

**Princess**    What's the sound of pee? Do it again.

**Yimoon**    *Sheeeeee – – – –*

**Princess**    *Sheeeeee*? Why am I not laughing?

**Yimoon**    Pretend you are peeing and simultaneously let out a long sound. *Sheeeeee – – –*

**Princess**    *Sheeeeee – – – – – –*

*Bursts out laughing.*

*Sheeeeee – – – – – –*

**Scene Thirteen**

Setting: **Gahkbi**'s Room.

**Gahkbi** *crouches down and looks at the moon through the door crevice.*

*She looks lost.*

**Gahkbi**   *Sheeeeee – – – – – –*

*She holds out her hand to catch the moonlight.*

The moonlight goes through my fingers. I caught it. Hey, where did it go?

*Stands up and tries to catch the moonlight.*

*(Suddenly.)* Oh, I'm all wet.

*Takes off all her clothes and chases the moonlight.*

**Hyunduk** (*enters*)   Gahkbi. Where have you been all day?

**Gahkbi** (*smiles with a silly grin. The moonlight through the door crevice gets in her eyes*)   How pretty. Brother, catch the moonlight for me.

**Hyunduk**   How embarrassing.

*He tries to put her clothes on her.*

**Gahkbi**   They're all wet. With pee.

**Hyunduk**   You peed on yourself again? What's wrong with you these days?

**Wooreuk** (*offstage*)   Is that Gahkbi? Where on earth have you been?

**Hyunduk** *clothes* **Gahkbi** *in a hurry.*

**Wooreuk** (*enters*)   You should tell us where you're going. The little one won't stop crying, looking for his mommy.

**Hyunduk**   She was picking sprouts up on the mountain.

**Wooreuk**   Picking sprouts this late at night?

**Gahkbi**   Right at the narrow slope. That's where I spotted a fox den. No mother, though, only the cubs. I asked Chanwoo to fetch them for me, but he was just so stubborn for a little one . . . I'm so wet.

*Takes off her clothes.*

**Wooreuk**   What are you doing?

**Hyunduk** (*he is surprised and tries to put her clothes back on her*)   They must have gotten dirty while picking sprouts.

**Gahkbi**   It's my pee. You don't know anything. I didn't pick sprouts. I saw a fox den. I'm going fox hunting with Chanwoo tomorrow. (*Exits.*)

*Silence.*

**Hyunduk**    Gahkbi's been acting bizarre lately. I'm afraid she's lost her mind.

**Wooreuk**    Ugh – Look at the state of this household. With the country fallen apart, how can a household stay together? You useless imbecile, you can't even take care of your sister. Hey, Gahkbi, Gahkbi! (*Exits.*)

**Hyunduk** *gets* **Gahkbi***'s clothes from the floor and folds them neatly.*

*He suddenly sobs.*


**Scene Fourteen**

Setting: The Palace.

**Yimoon** *is playing the* gayageum, *and* **Sangsa** *is sitting next to him.*

**Sangsa**    We are in the enemy's palace.

**Yimoon** *stops playing.*

**Sangsa**    Did you already forget how your parents died?

**Yimoon**    I'm alive. Life is meant to be enjoyed.

**Sangsa**    Master is waiting.

**Yimoon**    The Gayan musician is long gone. I am now a Silla musician.

**Sangsa**    . . . Gahkbi had your child. He must be about three or four by now.

**Yimoon** *is surprised, looks at* **Sangsa**.

**Sangsa**    Let's go back. The child deserves to know his father.

**Yimoon**    . . . . . .

**Sangsa**    You said you'll be in big trouble if they find out you're from Gaya. You had your fun here. Now let's get out.

**Yimoon**    The princess is deaf, and she trusts me.

**Sangsa**    What if she gets suspicious?

*Takes out a pouch from his sack.*

Take this medicine. It's strong enough to put anyone to sleep for at least a couple of days. If anything goes wrong, feed it to her and run.

*Offstage, the* **Princess** *is calling* **Yimoon**.

**Yimoon** *quickly puts the pouch in his pocket.*

**Yimoon**    It's the princess. Head to the floor.

**Princess**    A guest. Who is it?

**Sangsa** *kneels and puts his head to the floor*

**Yimoon**   I recruited another musician.

**Princess**   You're working hard.

**Yimoon**   You're wearing a helmet.

**Princess**   It's a new one. Molded with the iron from Yacheon.[28] It's so light even I can wear it. Examine this fine Silla iron.

**Yimoon**   You look like a general commanding thousands of troops and horses.

**Princess**   How does a general command? Like this? Hey! March! Oh, I learned how to laugh like a general. *Hahahahahahaha –*. You said to shake my head. (*Shakes her head.*)

*Hahahahahahaha* – Like this?

**Yimoon**   Exactly.

**Princess**   Since you taught me how to laugh, I will give you a present.

*She hands him* The Book of Sounds *from the Qin Dynasty.*

**Princess**   *The Book of Sound*s from the Qin Dynasty. I hear it contains everything about eccentric sounds and musical instruments from all over the world.

**Yimoon** *greedily opens the book and examines it. The* **Princess** *temptingly looks at* **Yimoon** *and pulls the book back towards her.*

**Princess**   Tell me why you desire this book.

**Yimoon**   I'd like to learn about musical instruments from other countries and how to play them.

**Princess**   Your desire is as deep as the ocean. But listen, Yimoon. This book should be kept hidden. This is no ordinary book that anyone can gain access to. You can learn about the *jamyeonggo,*[29] the drum that defeats the enemy, and the rain maker, which brings rain in a drought. A musical instrument is a capricious and evasive thing. If you lose even a single page, I will discipline you severely. Is that clear?

**Yimoon**   Yes, princess.

**Princess**   So, what sound will you teach me today?

**Yimoon** (*hands the book to* **Sangsa**)   Keep this safe.

**Sangsa**   Yes.

*Puts his head to the floor.*

**Yimoon**   Since your hands have become tender, I will teach you how to play the Gayan instrument *goh*. This is the *goh*.

**Princess**   That's the instrument that makes the sound of the moon.

**Yimoon**   Correct. The sound is so wondrous that people used to say it built a bridge between the earth and the sky. That God would descend on that very bridge.

**Princess**    Its bridge is silk threads on a piece of wood. How can it hold God? God deserves at least an iron bridge.

**Yimoon**    Excuse me? (*Laughs.*)

**Princess**    You're laughing now.

**Yimoon**    Oh, my deepest apologies.

**Princess**    I like seeing you laugh. Is your excitement tickling your lungs?

**Yimoon**    Yes, princess. The book you brought me made me very excited. (*Laughs.*)

**Princess**    Your laughter makes me happy. . . Yimoon. Did I just say I was happy?

**Yimoon**    Yes, princess.

**Princess**    Soon I will learn what it means to cry. All thanks to you. Once I learn that, I will appoint you as the court's master musician.

**Yimoon**    I am beyond grateful.

**Princess**    Today's lesson will be in my bedchamber.

**Yimoon** *and the* **Princess** *exit.*

**Sangsa**, *left alone, goes through the book.*

*He carefully looks around and suddenly tears pages from the book.*


**Scene Fifteen**

Setting: **Gahkbi**'s Yard.

*At the back of the stage, the* **Shaman** *is sitting, offering a ritualistic chant to the Spirits.*

*At the front of the stage,* **Gahkbi** *is sitting, laughing in a silly manner, and* **Yooldo** *is tying a rope around* **Gahkbi***. He is carefully eavesdropping on* **Wooreuk** *and* **Hyunduk***.*

**Wooreuk**    They must be from Silla. No shaman in Gaya would use a rope in an exorcism.

**Hyunduk**    Gaya or Silla, what does it matter? They say they can cure Gahkbi. So let's give them a chance. They say she is possessed, and an exorcism can bring her back.

**Wooreuk**    Possessed! That's nonsense. She brought this on herself. Her mother was like that, too. Hot-tempered. If she couldn't have her way, she would go insane.

**Hyunduk**    You left her on her own for way too long. Who could she turn to, who could she trust?

**Wooreuk**    Are you saying this is all my fault?

**Hyunduk**　. . . I'm sorry.

**Yooldo**　Let me tell you why we are tying her up. The exorcism will frighten the spirit and evict it from her body, but the spirit might enter another body or might hide for a while and enter her body again, so that's why we tie her up. This is a secret method practiced only by Gaya shamans, and we don't show it to just anyone. We actually learned it specially from the shaman who resides in the forest in Goryeong Gaya, a frightful place where none would dare to enter. Now we shall begin. . . We shall begin.

**Hyunduk**　Please do.

**Yooldo**　. . . A little offering for our trouble will do you good.

**Wooreuk**　Didn't we already pay for the service?

**Yooldo**　You paid for the service but not for the trouble.

**Hyunduk** (*disregarding* **Wooreuk**'*s anger*)　Here, take it.

**Yooldo**　That's all? I can hear the Spirit laughing.

**Hyunduk**　Once you cure Gahkbi, I'll give you more.

**Yooldo**　Hmm, she's got it really bad.

*Hits* **Gahkbi** *with a vine.*

**Gahkbi**　Ouch! What's that for?

**Yooldo**　See? The Spirit responds.

*Examining how* **Wooreuk** *and others react.*

**Yooldo**　Hey, whose Spirit are you? Gahkbi, Gahkbi.

*Beats* **Gahkbi** *with the vine.*

**Yooldo**　Uh-oh, my shoulders are getting heavy, the spirits are descending. That's right, that's right, this house is possessed by evil spirits. (*Sings.*)

> Spirit of protection, hovering all over the streets
> Spirit of anxiety, all around town
> Spirit of fire and ashes, where there is fire
> Spirit of parting, on the road
> Spirit in mourning of her parents
> Guardian spirit on the floor
> Spirit of cloth hiding under the shelf
> Spirit moving from wall to wall
> Spirit of the mountain
> Spirit of the tree
> Spirit of the forest –

Ugh, the spirits are so strong they are weighing me down. This won't do. Bring more iron for our trouble. I'm doubling the price.

**Wooreuk**    What a greedy crook.

**Yooldo** (*points at* **Wooreuk** *and imitates a spirit voice*)    You – are the problem. Your sin caused your daughter's suffering, and you can't even spare some iron.

**Wooreuk** (*pushes away* **Hyunduk** *and snatches* **Yooldo** *'s vine and beats him with it relentlessly*)    You bastard, you crook! How dare you utter such insanity? (*To* **Gahkbi.**)

**Wooreuk**    You useless wench, you can't hold it together, and you let this crook treat you like a lunatic. Just end it all. You don't know anything. I am a master musician royally respected in the great Gaya. You don't know anything at all.

**Yooldo** (*hiding behind* **Hyunduk**)    You scoundrel, may a spirit possess you. No, that's not right. It's my fault, please forgive me.

**Hyunduk**    Father, you're going to kill him.

*He holds* **Yooldo** *tight. They run away together.*

**Wooreuk** (*still fuming*)    You don't know anything, you iron-greedy Silla dog. You deserve to be tiger meat! Scum! Phew! Spirit, if you're really there, show yourself! What have I done to deserve such an ordeal at this age? (*Out of breath.*)

**Gahkbi** (*possessed by* **The Spirit of Gahkbi's Mother**)    Hey husband, Gahkbi's father.

**Wooreuk**    . . . . . .

**Gahkbi**    Please untie me now. This rope from the pillar is tightening around my neck. I can't breathe. Husband, please forgive me. Please let me breathe. Gahkbi's father . . . I've been too lonely. The wind was hitting the window, yet you were nowhere near. They gave me a coarse-tooth comb, and it was so pretty. . . . . . Husband, please forgive me.

**Wooreuk**    Jaehee.

**Gahkbi**    I didn't know I'd miss you this much even after death. . . Husband, what shall we do about poor Gahkbi?

**Wooreuk**    Jaehee, please forgive me. I was a mad, hot-blooded youth – It's all my fault, Jaehee. (*Cries.*)

**Scene Sixteen**

Setting: The Palace.

**Yimoon** *is on his knees, bound with a rope.*

**Princess** (*enters screaming*)    I lost a handful of hair! And see these red spots on my face? I had these spots when my mother tried to kill me! What have you done to me?

**Yimoon**    I have nothing to do with it, princess.

**Princess**    Then why did you ask me for the Qin Dynasty sound book?

**Yimoon**    Curiosity.

**Princess**    Sangsa, bring the evidence.

**Sangsa** (*shows torn pages from the book*)    These pages are torn from the Qin Dynasty's *Book of Sounds*. Yimoon made me do it.

**Yimoon**    Sangsa, you traitor! How dare you covet my position?

**Princess**    They contain information about the *jamyeonggo*. What was your purpose for stealing the design for Nakrang Kingdom's *jamyeonggo*? Confess. (*Beats him.*)

**Yimoon**    I did copy from the book, but not that part.

**Princess**    So you admit it. You copied from the book.

**Yimoon**    But I never took any pages.

**Princess**    Traitorous worm, I was fond of you. Yet you've betrayed me! Who were you stealing for? I am deaf, so I can't hear the *jamyeonggo* anyway. If not for me, who was it for? (*Hits and kicks him.*) Where do you come from?

**Yimoon**    . . . . . .

**Princess**    Sangsa, where is Yimoon from?

**Sangsa**    He's from Gaya.

**Princess** (*beats* **Yimoon**)    I gave you garments made of silk. I gave you my wealth and honor and trust. And this is how you pay me back!

**Yimoon**    It's all lies. I admire you and love you.

**Princess**    Love?

**Yimoon**    Sangsa framed me. He's from Gaya, too. His jealousy caused this.

**Sangsa**    I committed a mortal sin. Please kill me now. (*Bows down.*)

**Princess** *takes out the medicine pouch that* **Sangsa** *had given to* **Yimoon**.

**Princess**    This poison was found in your room. You're the only person who has access to me.

**Yimoon**    That can't be. It's all lies!

**Princess**    Take out his eyes, make him deaf, and throw him out of the palace. The sound of Gaya has tainted the ears of Silla. If you spot Gaya musicians, arrest them.

**Voice** (*offstage*)    Yes, princess –

*Blackout.*

**Scene Seventeen**

Setting: **Gahkbi**'s Room.

**Wooreuk** *is combing* **Gahkbi***'s hair.*

**Hyunduk** *is playing music next to them and then stops to listen to them.*

**Gahkbi**    Comb it quick.

**Wooreuk**    Stay still. It's all tangled up I don't know what to do. You're old enough to comb your own hair.

**Gahkbi**    Oh, a day moon.

**Wooreuk**    It's a half-moon. It looks pale, like it's been hiding from the sun and got caught.

**Gahkbi**    Why a half-moon? A moon is round. Why change shape?

**Wooreuk**    A moon goes back and forth.

**Gahkbi**    Why?

**Wooreuk**    It's like Chanwoo's tooth, you lose one and a new one comes out. Leaves fall from a tree in autumn, but they return in the spring. Even the light blue leaves. . . The mind is just like that. One day it hurts so much you think you'll die, and then it gets better and you keep living. That's just life.

**Gahkbi**    I like the moon in the day. I hope it rises in the day from now on.

**Wooreuk**    The moon comes out at night.

**Gahkbi**    Why?

**Wooreuk**    To help people find their way. If they get lost at night, the moon guides them.

**Gahkbi**    It's day now.

**Wooreuk**    So it's useless. It works on a pitch-black night.

**Gahkbi**    Yeah.

**Wooreuk**    Don't give me such nonchalant answer. Your brother went crazy looking for you a few days ago.

**Gahkbi**    It hurts –.

**Wooreuk**    Alright, I'll be gentle.

*Indicates directions.*

At night, Gahkbi, the moon rises here and sets there. Our house is right here. So in the evening the moon is on our left, at night it's right above us, and at dawn it sets over there. That's how you can find your course.

**Gahkbi**    Okay.

**Wooreuk**   Did you really understand?

**Hyunduk** (*laughs*)   Do you really think she did?

**Wooreuk**   What? (*Laughs.*) Why'd you stop playing?

**Hyunduk**   I can't concentrate. I just feel so stupid. It's like I got lost in the middle of a moonless night.

**Wooreuk**   If you got lost, you should find your way. Gahkbi, it's all done. It's such a beautiful day, how about practicing music with your brother?

**Gahkbi** *shakes her head.*

**Wooreuk**   How about dancing?

**Gahkbi** *shakes her head.*

**Wooreuk** (*sighs*)   You've really fallen out with music.

**Gahkbi**   Where is Chanwoo? Hey, Chan. (*Exits.*) Chan!

**Hyunduk**   Father, what do you do when you get lost while playing the *goh*?

**Wooreuk**   Look at the moon.

**Hyunduk** *Laughs.*

**Wooreuk**   Nobody can know where they are unless they seek guidance from the moon and the stars. Everybody gets lost if they confine themselves inside.

**Hyunduk**   My stupidity keeps me from reaching your standard. And still, I've been working myself to the bone to master your music. How mortifying.

**Wooreuk**   It's been quiet with Chan playing outside. Gahkbi is lost, all my students are gone, and I'm left here old and lonely. But Hyunduk, I'm grateful and happy you're still here.

**Hyunduk**   . . . . . .

**Chanwoo** *is crying.*

**Wooreuk**   Chan is crying.

**Wooreuk** *exits.*

**Wooreuk**   Hey, Chan. Where are you?

**Hyunduk**   Everybody gets lost if they confine themselves inside. What sound can I find outside of myself?

*Closes his eyes.*

*Long silence.*

*Sound of water from a distance. An owl hoots every once in a while. Or there is the sound of bamboo leaves shaking.*

*The green bamboo leaves shine beautifully in the sunlight.*

**Hyunduk** *opens his eyes and starts playing.*

*The sun sets and the half-moon becomes clear.*

**Scene Eighteen**

Setting: A Road at Night.

*The* gayageum *sound continues.*

*Enter* **Yimoon***, with eyes bandaged and bloody ears, on a leash held by* **Sangsa***.*

**Yimoon**    It hurts.

**Sangsa**    It hurts? Oh, you can't hear me. . . . . . We'll never get there walking this slow. You used to be fast back in the day. I was always behind you. I was so jealous of you. Master would give all his attention to you, and Ghakbi only had eyes for you. Even Hyunduk would give his right arm for you. I, on the other hand, was like an extra, just doing chores around the house. The moon set. It's dark now. But you wouldn't know, 'cause you can't see. This darkness brings back memories. We shared a room as children. We lived in a dugout, before we built a place with thatch. Once master locked me alone in the dugout as punishment. Remember? There was no light. I thought the darkness was choking me. If you and Hyunduk didn't speak to me from outside, I would have fainted. That was the only time I liked you. . . . . . Everything I used was passed down from you. Gahkbi made clothes only for you. Even my musical instruments were yours first. Even the socks I'm wearing right now. Gahkbi made these for you, you know. . . How did you lose your shoes?

**Sangsa**    *Is about to take off his shoes but stops.*

It's alright. Just as much as you hurt other people, your bare feet deserve to be hurt. Have you ever been jealous? I doubt it. Since you've always been the best, you wouldn't know what jealousy feels like. It belongs to those who are always in need, but you wouldn't know about that. Master taught us to play from the heart, but his heart was set on you alone. More unbearable was Gahkbi, yeah, Gahkbi having eyes only for you. Those were people I loved, and they only loved you. (*Laughs.*) Come to think of it, if God was just, would innocent people lose their limbs and lives in the war?

**Yimoon** *falls down.*

**Sangsa**    Is the stony road hurting your bare feet? . . . . . . Look at you now. This is what your pride led you to.

*Long silence.*

**Sangsa** *helps* **Yimoon** *to his feet.*

**Sangsa**    I'm sorry, Yimoon. I ruined you. . . Yes, I hated you, but my jealousy caused all this. I couldn't be like you, no matter how hard I tried. You had everything I ever wanted. I wanted to kill you. That makes me a despicable evil bastard.

*Picks up* **Yimoon** *and places him on his back.*

**Sangsa**    Let me carry you, Yimoon. Since I ruined you, let me be your hands and feet.

**Yimoon** (*on* **Sangsa***'s back, he angrily hits him*)    I'm hungry!

**Sangsa**    I hear you, so let's get going. I can't carry you for a month. Let's get you home before the moon turns full. We cross that mountain, and Gahkbi and Master will be waiting for us. We'll be back in Gaya again.

*They walk.*

*Blackout.*


**Scene Nineteen**

Setting: The **Princess**' Chamber.

*Solemn music like in a royal religious ceremony.*

*The* **Princess**, *in a magnificent crown and attire, is sitting with a* goh *in front of her. A* **Servant** *attends her.*

**Princess** (*fingering the strings*)    So you "pluck" the strings. I only began my lesson, and then it stopped. The hand playing the *goh* moves like a butterfly, which creates an elegant sound. . . . . . I miss you, Yimoon. My son finally became king, the crown I desired finally belongs to me, and yet I miss you more than ever. When my ears were poisoned as a child, it hurt like hell. Did it hurt, losing your eyes and ears? When Silla broke the agreement and attacked Gaya, I heard we even killed innocent women, children, and babies. How they must have hurt, dying like that. . . Oh, tears. I'm crying. (*Cries.*) I lost you and gained tears instead. . . . . . Listen. Set free all the imprisoned Gayan musicians. Since Silla occupied Gaya, Gaya is now part of Silla. Gayan musicians are now Silla musicians, and a *goh* from Gaya is now a *goh* from Silla.

**Servant**    Your Majesty. Since Gaya perished, its music has no value.

**Princess**    Gaya perished because of its immoral king. Its music is not to blame. I learned that good music comes from the heart. Let the Gayans who lost their country hear the *goh* and feel our benevolence. I will order a Gayan musician to play for King Jinheung[30] and publicize the king's benevolence across the nation. This *goh* will be called the *gayageum* from now on, and all Gayans will be treated as Silla citizens.

*Solemn and beautiful music plays like in a royal religious ceremony.*


**Scene Twenty**

Setting: **Wooreuk**'s House.

**Sangsa** *has brought* **Yimoon** *back home and is updating* **Wooreuk**.

**Gahkbi** *is sitting on a terrace stone, absent-mindedly playing with a straw doll.*

**Sangsa**    And that's how Yimoon's life got ruined.

**Hyunduk**    Did you carry him all the way from Seorabeol Palace? You must be exhausted.

**Sangsa**    I'm grateful I could pay for my sins this way.

**Wooreuk**    Hey, Gahkbi. Yimoon is back.

**Gahkbi** (*looks blankly then returns to playing with her doll*)    Rabbit, rabbit.

**Sangsa**    What happened to her?

**Hyunduk**    She waited for Yimoon, that's what happened. . . Are you still interested in her?

**Sangsa**    I ruined a person out of jealousy. How can I face her? If you let me, I would like to be Yimoon's eyes and ears.

**Hyunduk**    What do you think, Father?

**Wooreuk**    All of my students are back, and that makes me happy. I've been seeing things and feeling weary lately, and I'm afraid my death is imminent. I would like to devote my remaining time to playing music and sharing it with the world. And I would like to do it with all of you. Hyunduk, bring the instruments.

**Hyunduk** *brings the instruments.*

*Upon receiving the instrument,* **Yimoon** *plays it vigorously.*

**Wooreuk** (*laughs*)    Yimoon, your progress is remarkable. You lost your eyes and ears, but your heart opened up. (*To the others.*) Let's keep up with him.

*They play together.*

*A bird, surprised, flies out from a bush.*

**Gahkbi** (*gets up suddenly*)    A bird!

*They all stop playing, except for* **Yimoon**, *and look at* **Gahkbi**.

**Gahkbi** (*while looking at the bird, she spots the moon and points at it*)    The moon – has – risen!

*She starts singing to* **Yimoon***'s music.*

**Wooreuk**    Gahkbi is finally one with the sound! . . . . . . *He-hey!*

*He ad-libs and keeps playing.*

*Everyone joins in playing, and* **Gahkbi** *sings and dances.*

*The moon has risen.*

*It's a full moon.*

*End of play.*

**Notes**

1   This character is Princess Jiso, the daughter of King Beopheung and Queen Bodo. She married King Beopheung's brother Ipjong and gave birth to a son named Sammaekjong, who was coronated in 540 CE at the age of seven. Because of her son's young age, Jiso acted as Regent from 541 to 551 CE. Queen Jiso's accomplishment includes the building of Heungryunsa Temple and the creation of works of literature and national history. Sammaekjong became King Jinheung, one of the greatest kings of Silla, and reigned until 576 CE.

2   Wooreuk is a musician from Gaya. Details about his life are unknown. He created the musical instrument the *gayageum* upon the order of King Gasil. He is regarded as one of the top three Korean musicians, along with Wang San-ak from Goguryeo and Bak Yeon from the Joeson Dynasty.

3   The *gayageum* is a traditional Korean musical instrument with twelve strings, which are picked with the fingers. The right hand usually plucks the strings, while the left hand adds vibrato and other effects. The *gayageum* is known for its clear and elegant sound. It was originally called *gayago* or *gayatgo*. In this play, characters refer to it as *goh*.

4   Silla was a Korean kingdom that was established in 57 BCE and occupied the eastern part of the Korean peninsula. Silla formed the Three Kingdoms of Korea along with Goguryeo and Baekje. In 668 CE, Silla unified Korea and became the Unified Silla Dynasty, which lasted until 935 CE.

5   Gaya was a Korean confederacy of territorial states in the Nakdong River basin in southern Korea that was established in 42 CE and lasted until 562 CE, when it was absorbed by the Silla Kingdom.

6   The Qin Dynasty, 221–206 BCE, was China's first unified state with centralized power. Its founder, Ying Zheng, declared himself to be "Shi Huangdi," the first emperor of China. The Qin Dynasty established the administrative system, which all the subsequent dynasties were to follow for the next two thousand years. The name "China" is derived from Qin. The playwright mentions that Qin Dynasty symbolizes, in the world of this play, a prestigious ancient world full of treasures such as *The Book of Sounds* and *jamyeonggo* (which appear later in the play).

7   King Beopheung reigned from 514 to 540 CE. He is known for making Buddhism the state religion.

8   Garak is an alternate name for the most commonly used name Gaya, a Korean confederacy which existed during 42–532 CE. It was located in the Nakdong River basin in southern Korea. Gojami is one of Gaya's city states and is also referred to as Sogaya (small Gaya) or Goja State, located in the county of Gosung. The name Gojami can be translated as "a promontory related to water."

9   *Goh* also refers to the *gayageum*.

10   소슬바람: The gentle breeze that blows in autumn, which inspires feelings of loneliness and melancholy.

11   King Gasil of Gaya reigned as King of Gaya from the early-to-mid-sixth century. According to *Samguksagi* (the history of The Three Kingdoms of Korea, 1146), King Gasil, after having observed the ancient Chinese instrument *guzheng*, ordered Wooreuk to create the twelve-stringed instrument *gayageum*, and to compose twelve pieces. *Twelve Songs of Wooreuk* is titled after twelve of the city-states in Gaya and reflects each of the city-states' unique spirit and characteristics. The King's intention was to unite the kingdom through music.

12   사물(思勿): The fifth of the twelve *gayageum* pieces that Wooreuk composed. It is said that Wooreuk rearranged a folk song from South Gyeongsang Province.

13  Translator's Note: Gahkbi is jokingly imitating Wooreuk, identifying him with the sound of the moon, and Sangsa is playing along.

14  Seorabeol was the capital of Silla. Now named Gyeongju, it is a coastal city in the North Gyeongsang Province.

15  Goryeong Gaya was one of the lesser chiefdoms of the Gaya confederacy during the Three Kingdoms of Korea period. It was centered in present-day Sangju in North Gyeongsang Province, South Korea. Legend indicates that it was founded by King Taejo, whose tomb is located on Obong Mountain in Hamchang-eup, Sangju.

16  Gaya was known for its iron production, as the Nakdong River had rich iron deposits. Gaya exported iron ore, as well as iron armor and other weaponry, to Baekje. Iron, for this reason, was apparently regarded as a valuable currency.

17  This song is reminiscent of *samul nori*, which is traditional Korean folk music played with four instruments: *Kkwaenggwari* (a small gong); *Jing* (a larger gong); *Janggu* (an hourglass-shaped drum); and *Buk* (a barrel drum similar to the bass drum).

18  *Kalopanax septemlobus* is a deciduous tree native to Northeastern Asia.

19  This is an unofficial Korean custom of letting luck decide one's fate. Another example of finding direction based on luck is done with spit. One would spit in one's hand and hit the spit with the other hand. Wherever the spit flies indicates the direction one would choose.

20  Yooldo mistakenly assumes that Sangsa is the shaman.

21  Based on *Samguk Sagi* (History of the Three Kingdoms, the oldest surviving chronicle of Korean history), the Nakrang Kingdom is believed by Korean scholars to have been an independent nation. Chinese and Japanese scholars claim that the Nakrang Kingdom refers to the Lelang Commandery of the Chinese Han Dynasty.

22  A common Korean expression. When someone says something silly, absurd, or outrageous, you can say "a dog walking by will laugh at that."

23  Queen Bodo was the first wife and Queen of King Beopheung, the twenty-third king of Silla, who reigned from 514 to 540 CE, continuing the Kim clan's reign over Silla. She is known to have entered the Buddhist priesthood, following her husband who made Buddhism the state religion and entered the priesthood himself late in his life. Her contribution to the development of Buddhism in Silla is noted.

24  Pak Hyeokgeose was the founding monarch of Silla and the progenitor of the Park (Pak, Bak) clan, one of the most widespread clans in Korea, along with the Kim and Lee clans. According to *Samguk Sagi* and *Samguk Yusa*, which document the history of the Three Kingdoms in Korea, legend has it that Hyeokgeose was born out of an egg. The egg appeared in a forest in Yangsan, at a well called Najeong, in 69 BCE, on a day when a strange light shone from the sky. That year, six chieftains, who were refugees from Gojoseon, discussed forming a kingdom and, when one of them discovered the birth, they decided to make him king. Pak was made king in 57 BCE, when he was thirteen.

25  Michu of Silla: The thirteenth ruler of Silla and the first king of the Kim clan in Silla. Michu reigned from 262 to 284 CE. The Kim clan would rule Silla for most of its later history.

26  Naemul of Silla: The seventeenth ruler of Silla and the nephew of King Michu. Also married to Michu's daughter Lady Boban. He reigned from 356 to 402 CE.

27  The princess is the kingdom's regent because her father is in a monastery. She is worried that her father's second wife could still bear a son to replace her.

28  Yacheon: One of the rivers running down from the Gaya Mountain to the Nakdong River into Goryeong Country, the center of the ancient Kingdom of Daegaya.

29  The *jamyeonggo* is a legendary drum from the Nakrang Kingdom. It was believed that the drum possessed mysterious power to beat on its own when there was an enemy invasion. Some believe this self-sounding drum refers to an alarm system.

30  King Jinheung was the twenty-fourth monarch of Silla and reigned from 540 to 576 CE.

# The Wind's Desire

바람의 욕망

A full-length drama

By Myung-Wha Kim
Translated from Korean into English by Walter Byongsok Chon
English Language Translation Consultant: Anne M. Hamilton

© 2020–2026 by Byongsok Chon
All rights reserved

* The Korean production of *The Wind's Desire* premiered at the Sanwoollim Theatre in South Korea under the direction of Young-Woong Lim in 2007.

* An excerpt from this translation was presented at Ithaca College's series Fine Artists @ 5 on June 12, 2020, and the 2020 ATHE (Association for Theatre in Higher Education) conference.

* Scene Two of this translation was published in *Another Chicago Magazine* in May 2021.

* This play has been translated with official permission from the author. The contract is available upon inquiry.

* The Daesan Foundation awarded a 2022 Grant for the Translation of Korean Literary Works to Walter Byongsok Chon and Anne Hamilton to create *An English Theatrical Translation of Korean Plays by Myung-Wha Kim*. This collection of four plays includes several genres exploring Korean history, culture, and sentiments, thereby enhancing intercultural theatrical exchange. Walter Byongsok Chon is the translator and Anne Hamilton is the English language translation consultant. The collection includes *Birds Don't Use a Crosswalk*, *Oedipus: The Fate of the Story*, *Sound of the Moon*, and *The Wind's Desire*.

* The translator and English language translation consultant were each awarded a Fellowship by the Bogliasco Foundation, and completed Spring 2024 Residencies in Bogliasco, Italy. *An English Theatrical Translation of Korean Plays by Myung-Wha Kim* was created with the support of a Bogliasco Foundation Fellowship.

Walter Byongsok Chon

© 2020–2026 by Byongsok Chon

All rights reserved

## Characters

**She**  *Middle-aged, television writer, married with a daughter, a "wild goose mom."*[1]

**He**  *Twenties, photographer.*

**Friend**  *Female, middle-aged, television producer.*

**Superintendent**


## Time and Place

Present

Officetel – is a multi-purpose building with residential and commercial units. This is a type of studio apartment or studio flat.

The National Assembly Building Park in Yeouido – equivalent of the Capitol Building in Washington, DC in the United States where federal legislators conduct official government business. In the United Kingdom the equivalent is UK Parliament.

*Patbingsu* Bar – Korean dessert bar.

*Cheongju* Bar – Korean rice wine bar.


## Scenes

1. His Officetel
2. The National Assembly Building Park in Yeouido
3. His Officetel
4. *Patbingsu* Bar
5. His Officetel
6. *Cheongju* Bar
7. Her Officetel


## Notes on the Text

\* The translation follows the original text's punctuation as much as possible in order to reflect the original language's pacing and the author's intention. The ellipses ". . . . . .", ". . .", and "–" appear in the Korean text.

> Note: In Western script notation, the playwright's use of ". . . . . ." can be interpreted as being similar to a (*Pause.*).
> Accordingly, ". . ." is similar to a (*Beat.*).
> And "–" is similar to a breath.

* Notes provide explanations of specific Korean references for the reader's convenience.

**Content Warning**

*This play contains drinking, smoking, gaslighting, domestic violence, and physical intimacy.*

## Scene One

Setting: His Officetel.

*His office and living space.*

*One side leads to the entrance, the other to the bathroom.*

*The stage design of the bathroom has translucent walls, which sometimes makes the inside visible.*

*Once the stage lights up,* **She**, *in a bathrobe, is trying to open a wine bottle.*

*The bottle opener, which is possibly cheap, makes the task difficult.*

**She** *puts a cigarette in her mouth.*

*But* **She** *cannot find the lighter.*

**She**   The toils of everyday routine. The wine cork that wouldn't come out, the drawer that wouldn't open, locating a keyhole in the dark, no battery left when making an important phone call, and putting a cigarette in your mouth but not finding a lighter.

**She** *gives up the cigarette and dries her hair with a towel.*

There are worse things. A writer who needs to write but can't, a life that needs to be lived but has no purpose, and time that goes by and repeats itself with no apparent reason. The third clown who fell from the rope. I am that clown.[2]

**She** *tries opening the wine bottle again.*

*Eventually, the cork pops open with a loud pop.*

**She**   We bought wine but had no bottle opener. Was it our honeymoon? We giggled ourselves to exhaustion using chopsticks.

**She** *pours wine in her glass.*

Cheers to the comfort a glass of wine brings!

**She** *gulps down the wine.*

Not bad for a cheap brand. It must have been drawn from the trees and grown through sunshine, thunder, and rain, for this very moment. Then in the darkness and despair of the oak barrel, through sourness and loneliness, gradually ripening in tranquil resignation . . . . . . I smell lilacs.

**She** *picks up the wine glass, rises, and slowly wanders around.*

**She**   Things that make me happy. The clear sound when you pour the first glass of wine, the hot sensation from the liquor going down your throat, the scent of early spring flowers, and the crisp feeling of the air right before darkness sets in. Being carefree and not having to know what time it is, the touch of wet hair on my shoulder . . . . . . Spending a night in a strange place.

*Sound of water from the bathroom. Sound of singing in a deep voice.* **She** *listens to the song.*

He's singing. Maybe he feels good.

**She** *finds the lighter.*

There's the lighter. Never there when I need it, but there when I forget about it.

**She** *absent-mindedly switches the lighter on and off a few times.*

*A cell phone rings all of a sudden.*

**She** *is startled, takes out her cell phone from her bag, checks the phone number, and breathes a brief sigh of relief.*

**She**   Hello? . . . Yes, I'm fine. Meeting people is just such a fuss . . . No, I'm not home. Just taking a walk. Dinner? Something simple. That's what's nice about living alone . . . It's a treat for him, too, living without his wife in a strange land. He's got lots of friends in L.A. . . . . . . Worry, no. I wish he would date someone. I was planning to go to Yeouido[3] sometime next week anyway. I have to work hard to send money to the U.S.

**He** (*sound of the bathroom door opening*)   What? Did you say something to me?

**She** (*covering her phone*)   No –

*Back to her phone.*

I have to go. I'm boiling water for coffee. No, not boiling coffee but water for a coffee mix. I spilled some so I have to go. Let's talk later. Okay. Bye.

**She** *hangs up.*

*Silence.*

**She** (*fanning herself with her hands*)   Doesn't he have a fan? I can't find anything useful in this place. The furniture's all misplaced and mismatched . . . . . . What the hell am I doing here?

**She** *becomes self-conscious looking at herself in the mirror.*

**She**   Another white hair.

**She** *takes out her makeup kit from her bag and starts putting on makeup.*

**She**   Would my husband mind if I get plastic surgery? . . . That sounds like fun. A wild goose couple[4] reunites at the airport and hugs each other, and then the child says. "Dad, Mom's over there." (*Laughs.*) He couldn't possibly have called home last night . . . If I didn't pick up, he would have tried my cell.

**She** *finishes the makeup and checks herself on the mirror again.*

**She**   Virginia Woolf said. "Here the soul, getting restive . . . is variable as a weathercock."[5] Mrs. Woolf, I agree. My mood is different before and after I use the bathroom, and before and after I do my makeup. How about that? Not bad, right?

**She** *decisively ties her hair upward and puts on her clothes that were all over the floor.*

**He** *comes out of the bathroom and watches her.*

**He**    Hey. You alright?

**She**    Oh, my goodness.

**He**    Sorry. Did I scare you?

**She**    It's alright. No problem. A friend called me, and we talked for a bit.

**He**    Oh, okay.

*There is a silence between them, and* **He** *shyly puts on his clothes.*

**She**    What's with this awkwardness? Didn't we just make passionate love?

**He**, *fully dressed, acknowledges her and smiles.*

**He**    Did you have wine?

**She**    Sorry. I opened it without your permission. I was in the mood.

**He**    That's alright. I wasn't going to drink it alone, and I don't even know whether it tastes good. So I bought it just for decoration. Shall we have some?

**He** *hands her a glass.*

**She**    . . . . . . I was about to leave.

**He**    Now?

**She**    I have to be somewhere.

**She** *puts on her jacket.*

Why am I lying? I don't have to be anywhere. I go home, and I'll be alone. I can stay here a little longer.

**He**    There is still so much wine left. It's not that the wine will be wasted. But if you leave like this . . .

**She**    I'll take off now. I don't want to be late.

**She** *gets up.*

**He** *suddenly feels sorry about her leaving.*

**He**    Just a moment . . . This, this is my business card. In case you need to contact me or something.

**She**    Thank you. If anyone needs a photographer, I'll make sure to recommend you . . . Or is that not appropriate because you work for a magazine?

**He**    I'm a freelancer, so it will be okay.

**She**    . . . . . . About yesterday, I hope we can forget about it. Let's keep it to ourselves . . . Last night was a mistake.

**He**    A mistake?

**She**    We were drunk and got carried away, so let's not let it linger with us. We are adults, you and I. I have to go . . . I promise, I will recommend you.

**He**    Oh, okay. I appreciate that. This assignment, being your photographer, actually happened by chance. There was an accident, and I was the alternative. There are so many photographers nowadays, but not much work for those with insufficient experience. As you know, most young people take up unstable freelancing.

**He** *laughs.*

Good word of mouth can help me a lot.

**She** *gives a short nod and exits.*

*Silence.*

**He** (*finds her scarf and is about to go after her*)    Hey, you left this.

**He** *opens the door and closes it.*

Wait, hold it. If I run after her, I will look desperate. What about the scarf? I'll return it later. She said she'd keep me in mind for jobs. If she doesn't call, I can use the scarf as an excuse to call her myself. Call her? Should I call her first? Am I crazy? Because she left her scarf . . . . . . What is wrong with me? Why do I feel so dissatisfied and awkward, like I put on pants but forgot my underwear? That lady, could she be a player? Her leaving like this makes it look like we got drunk and screwed around.

**He** *lays out her scarf on the table and takes a picture of it.*

*Blackout.*


**Scene Two**

Setting: The National Assembly Building Park in Yeouido.[6]

*Sound of birds.*

**She** *is describing to her* **Friend** *the plot of her TV show.*

**Friend**    What's the age difference?

**She**    Twenty years . . . . . . Is it too shocking that he could be her son?

**Friend**    Another writer did that already. Mi-Kyung Choi had a hit with it. One show like that is enough.

**She**    A drama requires adultery and revenge. You said you needed a hit.

**Friend**    It still has to be acceptable. But she is twenty years older? Viewers don't get tired of the opposite. That's the way it is in real life.

**She**    So?

**Friend**   It doesn't work the other way. They like it the first time. Because it looks fresh and subversive. It's finally okay to portray the suppressed desire of women. But they're already fed up the second time around. You like a steak once in a while, right? But try it for lunch and then again for dinner. You get tired of it.

**She**   I'm not talking about desire. I'm talking about love.

**Friend** (*sighs*)   Talking about love at your age. Is she his stepmother, by any chance? Like in *Phaedra*? Even in a TV show, our viewers expect a certain quality.

**She**   He's a photographer.

**Friend**   Who is?

**She**   The main character. She gives an interview for a magazine, and he later takes her around town taking photographs. It suddenly pours, and they run out of the palace, under one umbrella. Sounds good, right? They take shelter under the leaves, their eyes meet, and they feel awkward. They go out for dinner, get drunk, and have sex that night.

**Friend**   What does she do for a living?

**She**   She's married. A writer. No, that's not fun. I don't know yet. I didn't get that far.

**Friend**   The main character's profession makes or breaks the show. Let's make her a doctor or a lawyer. Actors get pretentious when they play a writer or an artist.

**She**   You're the queen of finding fault.

**Friend**   So a one-night stand, drunk on rain. Then love?

**She**   Can it work like that?

**Friend**   Maybe for him, but what about her?

**She**   Well. (*Fanning herself.*) She senses that her life took a wrong turn at some point. Like when you start with the wrong button on your shirt, everything falls apart. Now she feels the emptiness, the loss, that she's not young anymore and has lived her life the wrong way.

**Friend**   That's not love.

**She**   . . . . . .

**Friend**   A middle-aged woman feels empty. And she desires a young man. That's yearning for the return of spring. Love takes more than that. A love that's like destiny, that pierces the soul – that's what gets the viewers' attention. Falling passionately in love at first sight. Or intense craving. But what would you know about love?

**She**   Hey. Why wouldn't she, at age fifty?

**Friend**   That's not enough. Add some ingredients.

**She**   Like what?

**Friend**    Like ties to social issues. If you can't change her, change him. That's it. Most young people take up unstable freelancing nowadays. They have to earn a living. Men tend to have stronger survival instincts than women. The woman craves sex because she's not getting any from her husband, and the man's in need of a stepping stone. He should have lots of credit card debt. He threatens to tell her husband and demands money.

**She** (*sighs*)    Here she goes again. Why does she always add and calculate and make it vulgar? She's been nagging me like this since we teamed up at the college broadcasting station. Dear Lord, why are you doing this to me? I already have a husband who nags me.

**Friend**    Do you know what your problem is? You don't get what it's like in reality. Have you been involved with anyone else besides your husband? Imagine you are your heroine. Can you spend a night with a random young man? And would he fall for you and keep seeing you? You say he's twenty years younger.

**She**    Is it impossible?

**Friend**    For me, no. But absolutely for a prude like you.

**She**    . . . . . . Are you saying a prude can't love? It may start with craving but can slowly heat up into love. They keep seeing each other. She can't stop calling him. She believes it's just a one-night thing at first. She thinks she had fun. But she's going crazy yearning for him. Where she used to feel emptiness, there's love. She's burning with passion, and it totally messes her up. Would the viewers accept that?

**Friend**    I doubt it.

**She**    Everyone falls in love. But there's no such thing as endless love. She felt it briefly in her twenties, but that was it. Her husband is self-absorbed. It's not that there is no love between them. But her husband loves like a cookie-cutter, always the same, no more excitement. Since she falls in love again, she becomes more exciting and vibrant –

**Friend**    I get that's what happens to her. But can a Korean man love a woman twenty years older? In the Republic of Korea?

**She**    Well . . . I'm not quite sure about that, either. She feels that way for him. But why would he like her? It's hot.

**She** *fans herself with her hand.*

The weather's insane these days. Why so hot? Summer's still far away. Why are there so many tourists? I couldn't even enjoy the cherry blossoms without bumping into them.

**Friend**    You know the cherry blossoms bring the crowds to Yeouido. Is it that hot?

**She** *casts a side glance at her friend and stops the fanning.*

**Friend**    Isn't it quieter here? Many people know the National Assembly Building, but not many know about this park.

**She**    . . . . . .

**Friend**    Are you upset? I didn't mean to find fault with your story. But you know this business lives and dies with ratings. Frankly, the ratings for your last show were dismal. We're renewing your contract because we trust you. But the burden's on me as the Director of Programming. The failure of this one will put me in a difficult position. It'll need to get at least average ratings, if not more.

**She**    I didn't say anything.

**She** *'s hot again.* **She** *fans herself.*

**Friend**    Are you having your period regularly?

**She**    What are you talking about, all of a sudden?

**Friend**    Is it happening regularly, without too much or too little bleeding?

**She**    I guess it is.

**Friend**    Are you getting hot and then cold, with a burning sensation in your face? You keep fanning yourself. I don't feel that hot.

**She**    . . . . . .

**Friend**    It must be menopause. My older sister has similar symptoms. Now women in their mid-forties have menopause. There's too much stress. That's you right now. Your husband and daughter are in the U.S. And it's still not good with your husband?

**She**    We'll have been married for twenty years next year. Affection's been out of the picture for a while.

**Friend**    Is he making any money nowadays?

**She**    He's abroad with the kid, so how can he?

**Friend**    You don't have to yell, jeez.

**She**    Drafting my show's been stressing me out. I couldn't sleep last night.

**She** *suddenly gets up and looks down at Yoon Joong Ro.*[7]

*Sound of birds.*

*Change in lighting.*

**She**    What a sight. An avalanche of people, an avalanche of flowers. Once it rains, they'll all be gone. What were the cherry blossoms thinking, blooming so outrageously?

**Friend**    She's gained weight. She used to be so thin and plain. It's menopause. Her outburst is so intense now. She was manic before, but not like that.

**She**    How can I excuse myself from this meeting? She's so lucky. No human being in the history of the world has uttered everything that comes to her mind just like that. Then she'll act all nice and sweet, offering to buy me lunch or giving me a present from abroad. She'll definitely offer to buy me lunch today. What can I tell her? I'll get indigestion. Would she be upset if I tell her I have another meeting?

**Friend**  She's become so bitter since her husband's business collapsed. With her life hitting rock bottom, looking at me must be a blow to her self-esteem. How can I comfort her? We already have a contract, so I can't let her go. But will she give me what I need? She wrote period pieces before, but this is her first romance.

**She**  It's an inferiority complex. She didn't grow up in a normal household and had a miserable childhood. Her parents got divorced, her husband's cheating on her, and she's got nothing going on but her job. And I don't get what it's like in reality? That's fatal for a writer. Did I lose my sense of reality, writing period pieces all this time?

*Sound of birds.*

*The lighting changes again.*

**Friend**  Let's get lunch and celebrate our contract.

**She**  Huh? I actually . . . Okay, let's. The contract's signed, so it's my treat.

**Friend**  Let me. My husband got a promotion.

**She**  Really? . . . Congratulations.

**Friend**  What are you in the mood for? I'll treat you to whatever you're craving.

**She**  Well?

**Friend**  How about webfoot octopus?[8] They're in season. I know a good place nearby.

**She**  Webfoot octopus?

**Friend**  You haven't heard, "webfoot octopus for spring, baby octopus for fall"? Webfoot octopus is the best now. It's loaded with eggs and so scrumptious.

**She**  It feels wrong to eat something that's pregnant.

**Friend**  Life is cruel by nature. So you never tried it? The male has ink, and the female has tiny white eggs filling her head, which pop when you bite into them. It's marvelous. The spring weather's exhausting us, so let's have some webfoot octopus and get our strength back. And have *soju*.[9] My mouth is watering just thinking about it. Let's go.

**Friend** *drags her out.*

*A few cherry blossom leaves float around in the air.*

*Blackout.*


## Scene Three

Setting: His Officetel.

*Sound of rain.*

**He** *is drinking wine.*

*Long silence.*

*Sound of a key rattling.*

**He**   It's Odysseus. At long last, Odysseus enters.

*The door opens, and* **She** *appears in sunglasses and with a wet umbrella.*

**She** *is confident and energetic for a spring day.*

**He** *strides towards her and gives her a hug.*

**She** (*handing him the umbrella*)   I just about got out. My kid and husband are back for the summer break and are home all day long. I couldn't even send them out in the rain. Were you drinking wine?

**He** *hands her his glass.*

**She**   I got soaked between the parking lot and the entrance. I'm shivering . . . Around Hongdae[10] is basically a parking lot. It took me a full hour to get here.

**He**   You're two and a half hours late.

**She**   My daughter and I went to the department store to exchange her swimsuit.

**He**   I thought you were not coming.

**She**   How did your last project go? The editor is a junior colleague, and she likes your work.

**He**   The pay is too small. I expected a major publisher to pay better, so I purchased a new laptop with my credit card. But now I can't afford it.

**She**   The new model?

**He**   Could you buy it for me?

**She**   You're bankrupting me. I'm meeting my family for dinner soon. Did you shower? Come here. I don't have much time.

**She** *kisses him, and her cell phone rings.*

**He** *tries to keep going, but* **She** *stops him and picks up the phone.*

**He**   I waited two and a half hours.

**She**   Hello. Hi. I'm driving, so I can't talk right now, I'll call you back . . . . . . By next week? Hey, that's impossible. I'm not ready to show it to the sponsors yet. The way you take care of business is just . . . Okay, I'll do it. Just give me the email address. (*To* **He**.) Pen and paper. (*To* **Friend**.) How about Park Ju-Young? He's young, but he looks old. Shi-Ok is too fat. (*To* **He**.) Can you bring me a wine glass? (*To* **Friend**.) You can't hear me? Maybe it's the rain. I can hear you. Okay. Give me the email address . . . It's fine. I'm parked by the street.

**He** *hands her the wine glass.*

**She** *laughs pleasantly.*

**He**    Liar. Your car is not by the street but in the officetel parking lot. You were not driving but hugging and kissing me. You are completely disregarding my presence without even blinking an eye. What does that make me? A non-presence.

**She** (*gets up suddenly and talks to* **Friend**)    You called my house?

**She** *insecurely glances at him and then goes into the bathroom.*

You spoke to my husband? . . . . . . Yes, I told him I was seeing you about something. You should have made something up . . . My goodness. What did he say?

*Sound of rain.*

**He** *turns on his work light and prepares to work.*

**She** *comes out and cautiously checks his mood.*

**She**    I'm afraid I have to go.

**He**    . . . . . .

**She**    Are you angry?

**He**    . . . I waited for two and a half hours, and you're leaving as soon as you get here?

**She**    My daughter wants to exchange her swimsuit all of a sudden. She's leaving for camp tomorrow.

**He**    You couldn't give me a call?

**She**    I couldn't call you in front of my daughter. That's morally problematic.

**He**    Morals? (*Laughs.*) Fuck that. Do you keep any morals for my sake? You call anyone anytime when you're here. You pick up your phone while we're doing it. As if that's normal. Is that not morally problematic? How convenient.

*Silence.*

*Sound of rain.*

**He**    Can you pay attention to me for once? Today you have work, tomorrow you have family. Even here, your phone keeps ringing.

**She**    That's why I came to see you.

**He**    Don't act so confident. Do you know you always act too confident?

**She**    . . . . . .

**He**    Have you ever felt sorry for me?

**She**    . . . I'm sorry.

**He** *forces a smile and returns to his work.*

**She** (*to herself*)    I drove up here like crazy, like I was Lady Chatterley. And look how he's treating me. Inconsiderate bastard. I miss him so much that I'm not myself when

I'm with my family. And he wants me to feel sorry for him? . . . Confident. My husband told me the same thing. Why are you always so confident? What makes you so proud? (*Sighs.*) I hate to go home. What am I going to tell my husband? I went to the library to do some research? Or there was a writers' group meeting? I hate lying. I just want to be honest. I no longer want to be with you. I'm sick of your eyes, your mouth, your ears, your whole self . . . Society will call me insane for getting divorced at my age and dating a young man who can be my son . . . . It's pouring. The traffic will be bad.

**She** *hesitates then hugs him from behind.*

I'm sorry.

**He**   . . . . . .

**She**   I have to go. My husband might have found out.

**He**   Filthy.

**She**   What? How dare you . . .

**She** *picks up her bag and goes to the exit.*

**He** *forces her to the chair under his work light.*

**She**   Let go of me!

**He** *picks up the camera.*

**She**   I have to go –

**He**   Stay right there. You're not going anywhere until I get the picture I like.

**She**   Don't. I'm not in the mood.

**He**   Today you do what I say.

**She**   What are you going to do with those pictures?

**He**   I'll use them to blackmail you. I can do whatever I want with my woman. I'll post them on the internet if you don't do what I say.

**She** *tries to get up, and* **He** *tears open her blouse while trying to stop her.*

**He**   Don't act like you're better than me. You say all these decent things, but you always protect yourself. You don't give a damn about how I feel. Everything's up to you. And you don't feel remorse because you buy me stuff? You stink.

**She** (*slaps him hard*)   Don't act innocent. Buy you stuff? Who asked for them?

*Silence.*

*Sound of rain.*

**She** *slowly buttons up her blouse.*

*Her cell phone rings.*

**She** (*takes out her cell phone and turns it off*)   It's my husband.

**He** You should leave.

**She** *takes out a cigarette from her bag.*

*Sound of rain.*

*With the cigarette in her mouth,* **She** *returns to the seat under the light.*

**She** Take the pictures.

**He** . . . . . .

**She** Please make me pretty. I will use them for my funeral.

**He** *adjusts the angle of the light.*

**She** Why did you become a photographer? You said you studied painting.

**He** I wasn't good at painting . . . . . . When did you start smoking?

**She** In college.

**He** I noticed most women your age don't usually smoke, but professional women smoke a lot.

**She** It looked cool. Not like a sheltered girl from a prestigious family. That was important back then. Short cut hair, bare face, studying, discussing, and getting involved in world affairs, just like men . . . . . . For a long time, I didn't see myself as a woman. Is that why I'm so confident? Why I'm too proud to say I'm sorry?

**He** After my father died, I looked through his photo album. There was a picture, I think, of my first day in kindergarten. There was Father in an old-fashioned trench coat and, standing next to him, a little boy with a yellow kindergarten cap holding flowers. It felt strange. Everything fades away, leaving no trace. Yet this moment was etched in time.

**She** You liked your father.

**He** It was a normal relationship . . . Maybe that's when I got into photography.

**He** *starts clicking the shutter.* **He** *photographs her foot, her shin, her knee, her hand by the ash tray, her other hand on her knee, slowly from bottom to top, and from side to center. His photos of her are projected in the background.*

**She** Isn't it an odd angle?

**He** Yes.

**She** Are you doing it correctly?

**He** No.

**She** Why?

**He** I'll keep doing it, all night long if necessary, until I get just the exact facial expression I want from you. Don't raise your chin and stay still.

**He** *keeps clicking the shutter.*

*Sound of the camera shutter.*

*Blackout.*


**Scene Four**

Setting: Patbingsu[11] Bar.

**She** *and her* **Friend** *are having* patbingsu.

**Friend**    Seriously? Are you insane? Even if it is for your story, what are you doing having an affair with someone twenty years younger?

**She**    Keep your voice down.

**Friend**    So, whenever you were seeing him, you told your husband you were seeing me? Even the other night?

**She**    . . . . . .

**Friend**    Is he a student? Did he do his military service?[12]

**She**    I didn't ask him about the military service. He probably did it. He graduated from college. Don't worry. He's an adult. You should see your face. You look as if I've assaulted a minor.

**Friend**    What's his job?

**She**    A freelance photographer.

**Friend**    Photographer? Exactly like your story. Are you crazy? So your new story is all about you?

**She**    Do you think I'm an exhibitionist?

**Friend**    He's a photographer and twenty years younger.

**She**    Some parts are the same. But only some, and the rest is fiction. I don't want to write about life itself but how life makes me feel. How feelings can be truthful or confusing. This is not a peek into my diary.

**Friend**    But why a photographer? At least change his job.

**She**    Fine. I'll make the woman a photographer.

**Friend**    Don't make me laugh.

**She**    It's just . . . I like photography now.

**Friend**    How long has it been?

**She**    Since this spring. Not even six months.

**Friend**    Which came first?

**She**    I don't understand.

**Friend**    The writing or love? Did you by any chance approach him for your story?

**She** *dismisses her* **Friend**

**Friend**    That's it! Just like when you went all the way to that military town to expose that prostitution scandal.

**She**    Among all the things to bring up now.

**Friend**    Do you know how painful it was for your husband? His wife, right after marriage, and pregnant, frequents a military town. He got drunk and cried and questioned what he had gotten himself into.

**She**    I was new to this. I would have sold my soul to the devil for a story.

**Friend**    And now?

**She**    Nothing's permanent. Time goes by, and everything changes. My taste in food, my body, my hobbies. If the devil asks me now. I will not sell my soul for a story. Instead –

**Friend**    Instead, what?

**She**    I will sell my soul to return my body to my twenties. Right away.

**Friend**    Get a plastic surgery. Once you make a fortune.

*They laugh out loud.*

**Friend**    This is no laughing matter! I'm dead serious.

**She**    I know . . . Love is just like that. You think it's permanent, but it's not. You said you were happy with your husband, but he cheated on you for a long time.

**Friend**    You knew?

**She**    It's a small world. What's strange is, we all know love doesn't last forever. But still, when it comes to love, we get weak, sick, and confused.

**Friend**    Eat your ice. It's melting.

**She**    That's why I made him a photographer. Look at this ice. It's all gone now. That's life. Photographs give us at least some moments to remember. Some proof that love did exist, and it was true, even long after it's all gone.

*Silence.*

*The light changes, and they are having their* patbingsu.

*They are lost in their own thoughts, playing with their food using their spoons instead of eating it.*

**She** · Should I have kept this to myself? It would have been better confessing it to a complete stranger, like a fortune teller or a priest.

**Friend**    What do I do with her? Being so naïve at age fifty . . . And he's twenty years younger? Is she that attractive?

*Looking at her.*

**She**    What's with that piercing gaze? I bet she's never had a romance. Even her marriage was arranged.

**Friend**    How do I face her husband now? He's in Korea until late August. Will she keep using me as an excuse while seeing her boyfriend?

**She**    The ice is completely melted . . . How ugly it looks. I must look that to her. Like an ugly adulteress. I really shouldn't have shared this.

**Friend**    Is this better for her writing, though? You can't make up the affair she's having, so maybe it's helping her. She's been in decline for a while. Maybe this can bring her back . . . No, being hopelessly in love doesn't lead to good writing.

**She**    Why did I bring this up all of a sudden? Did I need an accomplice? Just to share my romance, my beautiful secret? . . . . . . Mirror, mirror, on the wall, who's the most romantic of them all? And the mirror answers. The most romantic of them all is . . . how stupid is this. I'm showing off my romance like a teenager.

*The light returns to normal.*

**Friend**    Don't you think it's too simple?

**She**    What is?

**Friend**    Your story. A love affair with twenty years of age gap having a happy ending. It just isn't realistic. Viewers will not accept an unbelievable ending.

**She**    Unbelievable? Do I not look believable to you? Are you hoping my relationship will fail?

**Friend**    What are you talking about? Hey, I'm talking about your story.

**She**    I know, my story. That's what I'm talking about, too. Why do you think it's impossible? Isn't that some kind of social prejudice?

**Friend**    Are you saying you can talk to your husband about this affair? Are you out of your mind? Are you willing to leave your family and make it work with that young man?

**She**    Where is *this* coming from? I thought we were talking about my story.

**Friend**    Yes, your story!

**She**    Then why do you mention my husband? You think you've got something on me. I shared my secret because you are my friend. And you're using it to provoke me.

**Friend**    You know what your problem is? You can't control your emotion when it matters. I can't even have a conversation with you.

**She**    The problem is with you. Do you always have to attack my Achilles' heel?

**Friend**    No, it's not that. I'm worried our show will be boring. There's no climax or reversal.

**She**    Boring? Have my shows been boring so far?

**Friend**    Let's stop this. Or we'll get into a fight.

**She**    Alright. Let's stop this.

*Silence.*

**Friend**    Don't worry too much. Your romance is none of my business. All I care about is our show. Your secret is completely safe with me, so you can relax. I will not even bring it up with you unless you mention it first.

**She**    I've been so tense, like a tight rubber band. It's like, every day, I'm riding a roller coaster to the top of the ride and then falling straight down.

**Friend**    Why wouldn't it be like that? You're married, and your lover's twenty years younger. I'd die of a heart attack.

**She**    Bitch, you said you wouldn't bring it up.

**Friend**    I know I did. Finish your ice, Miss Juliet.[13] It's melting.

**She**    . . . . . .

**Friend**    Go ahead. It's quite tasty.

**She**    Yeah. With simple toppings.

**Friend**    Right. Other *patbingsu* places put all kinds of fruit and ice cream on top and make it messy. You can't tell what you're eating. But here it's simple. There's red bean, there's ice, and a couple of rice cakes. The red bean seems store made. The ice is quite tender. Like frozen milk.

**She**    Just like love and marriage. Marriage adds too many toppings. You have to have a baby, take care of the in-laws, purchase a house, get insurance, save money, decide what to make for dinner, calculate when you're getting a raise, worry about the worn-out couch, make kimchi, and you suddenly wake up and think you're Alice in Wonderland. Why am I toiling through living with this man and sharing the same space? Who is this man who winces at my sight and doesn't give a damn when he burps during dinner?

**Friend**    That's life.

**She**    But romance gets rid of all the toppings and leaves only the lovers. The best quality ice and the best quality red bean. No room for anything else. Just a pure *patbingsu* . . . . . . What am I doing? I must be in love with him. I thought it was just a drunken mistake. I thought I'd give him some clothes, give him some pocket money, like paying a service fee, have some fun, and be done with it. But now I can't control how much I want to be with him. The thought that this is so wrong because of my husband and daughter keeps igniting my desire, and I don't know what to do about it.

**She** *cries.*

**Friend** *looks at her.*

**Friend**    Since when was she this pretty? The friend who used to be plain and stiff like an old tree is now dazzling like a spring flower . . . . . . Pretty, my ass. It's shameless at that age. Like always, impulsive and clueless in everything she touches. Does she think she's Juliet? What does she want from me, whining like a teenager? People at the next table are looking at us, and she should be embarrassed, making a scene like this . . . But why do *I* feel so old? Love? . . . What was that? . . . . . . The long, long nights waiting for a cheating husband, the boring meals with nothing to say to each other, or the weary evenings spread out over the couch watching TV together? Was that love?

**She** (*getting herself together and standing up*)    I think the people at the next table are looking at us. Let's go. This is my treat.

**She** *exits.*

**Friend** *gets up slowly, while looking in her direction.*

**Friend**    Did she use to dress so boldly?

*Observes her own plain suit.*

*Blackout.*

*Sound of cicadas.*


## Scene Five

Setting: His Officetel.

*Autumn.*

**He**    I was surprised, too.

**She**    You're just you, but I have a family.

**He**    I know.

**She**    What do you know? You're only twenty-nine. I just found out when a friend called me today. And I, the center of the gossip, am the last to hear about it. I'm fuming just thinking about all the whispering going around. You *knew* about this? Why didn't you call me?

**He**    You don't answer my calls.

**She**    For something like this, you should have found a way to reach me!

**He**    I was being careful. I never imagined it would come to this.

**She**    Careful? You call me twelve times a day or wait around in a café in my neighborhood. Is that being careful?

**He**    You keep avoiding me.

**She**    I told you I was too busy with my writing.

**He**    This continuous waiting was driving me crazy.

**She**    So that's why you spread this rumor? Or did you trade it for money?

**He**    . . . . . . What are you talking about?

**She**    My photos are all over the internet. The photos that you took.

**He**    They were already published in the magazine. They're easily searchable.

**She**    But why those pictures?

**He**    I didn't do it.

**She**    If not you, then who? You really didn't tell anyone about us?

**He**    I didn't.

**She**    Can you swear?

**He**    . . . . . .

**She**    Why do you hesitate?

**He**    I don't think I told anyone. But when I got drunk . . . I may have told my girlfriend.

**She**    Are you crazy?

**He**    I didn't say your name. It was just too hard and, I don't know. I don't remember how much I told her.

**She** *sighs.*

*Silence.*

**She**    He must not realize the magnitude of this. He's just getting started with his life. He has no idea what a fall from grace is. Plus, he's a man. For a single young man, being at the center of a scandal is like getting a medal. But what about me? This scarlet letter scandal will be the end of me.

**He**    I'm sorry.

**She**    What did you say about me?

**He**    I don't remember. I had a lot to drink that day. She was extremely upset . . .

**She**    Nice excuse. So you told her? Your own girlfriend of all people? Bastard. And you kept seeing your girlfriend while you were seeing me? No wonder those online articles were so hostile to me.

**He**    I didn't know it would come to this. I couldn't stand this double relationship. So to put an end to it, I had to tell the truth.

**She**    Truth? What truth?

**He**    You're the one I love. I'm glad this happened. Keeping this love a secret became unbearable.

**She**    Don't be naive. What we had was like the wind. Do you really think there is any truth in our relationship?

**He**    There was nothing?

**She**    . . . . . .

**He**    You didn't love me?

**She** *puts on the coat from the couch.*

**She**    So he loved me. Getting this confession at a moment like this. God, you are indeed almighty. I was afraid he was just fooling around with me. I fought with all my will to resist my emotion, to not be the only fool to fall in love. And he says he loved me? Love. With all this mess. What's the point?

**He**    She looks old today. Lots of white hair. Was her hair dyed beforehand?

**She** *fastens her coat and picks up her bag.*

**She**    Let's end this.

**He**    Really.

**She** *heads toward the entrance.*

*The doorbell rings.*

**She** and **He** *freeze like a still-life painting.*

*The doorbell rings again.*

**He**    Who is it?

**Superintendent** (*offstage*)    I'm glad you're home. This is the superintendent. Can I see you for a moment?

**He**    What do I do? Fuck. I shouldn't have answered.

**She**    Why is he here?

**He**    I don't know.

**She**    Ask him.

**He**    Is there a problem, sir?

**Superintendent** (*offstage*)    I need your signature.

**She**    He might be a reporter. Earlier today I got a call from a random reporter from a daily magazine I've never even heard of. He might have followed me. Don't open the door. What do I do?

**He**    Go hide in the bathroom. I'll keep him away.

**She** *heads toward the bathroom.* **He** *picks up her shoes and hands them to her. Sound of knocking on the door.* **She** *looks at him, scared, just as she enters the bathroom, and* **He** *gives her a nod.*

**He**    Okay. I'm coming.

**She** *closes the bathroom door. The stage and the bathroom go dark. A sound like a heartbeat is heard for a while and fades.*

**She**    What the . . .? Oh, the light! Shhh!

**She** *covers her mouth.*

. . . . . . It's too dark in here. Yes, there was a small lamp by the sink.

**She** *uses her finger to find the lamp.*

What the hell am I doing in this darkness? Punished, for desiring the forbidden fruit. God, please forgive me. God, who pities the weak and the foolish in this world, please pity this lost sheep. Please let this moment pass with no harm. Then I will start going to church. I will attend the Catholic mass and make donations. Oh! Found it.

*The lamp lights up.*

Thank you, God. The light will not give me away, right?

*Her face is reflected in the mirror under the lamp.*

Look at yourself. What am I doing here? How embarrassing it would be if the door flew open this moment. Did I lock the door? God, please turn me into a tiny mouse so that people can't spot me. No, I hate mice. I'd rather be a cockroach. God, please turn me into a cockroach. No, not a cockroach. Into a bacterium. I'm vermin. I'm a human worse than vermin.

*The light bulb goes out all of a sudden and makes a loud sound.*

Oh my!

**She** *covers her mouth.*

No, I can't scream . . . Did the light bulb have to go out right now? I don't think God is going to forgive me. Could they hear me out there? . . . I can't hear a thing. This must be soundproof. What do I do? I'm all over the internet, and everybody will recognize me now. Should I emigrate? No. I'm a writer. How can I abandon my language and live somewhere else? That's right. I got together with him to gather material for my story. I can say I needed to find out what it was like in order to write my story. At some point, that was the case. And that's why I dated this young man? . . . People will call me crazy. Adultery sounds less insane. But that term "adultery" is too horrific. It's so dark in here . . . . . . I have claustrophobia. What do I do?

*Long silence. All of a sudden,* **She** *takes out a Zippo lighter from her bag and lights it. Her silhouette gradually emerges out of the darkness.*

**She**    "The fire that can withstand a running train, Zippo lighter."[14] (*Laughs.*) I'm glad I didn't quit smoking. I am the Little Match Girl. Holding on to this lighter to get through this darkness . . . The tiles are pretty cold. The freezing chill is coming up through my hips.

*Long silence.* **She** *holds up the lighter and peers through the darkness. The light flickers.*

**She**    I remember being trapped in the dark like this when I was little. Mom locked me in the closet for coming home too late from my friend's. My begging and crying had no effect on her. In the closet it was dark and tight. Pitch black. Like the darkness would never let me see the light again. There was a weird smell. Probably naphthalene. It was suffocating . . . . . . Was it like this at the Sampoong Department Store collapse?[15] The girl who narrowly escaped death said something like this. In the darkness, she couldn't feel the passing of time. I should look up that story once I'm out of here. Despair in darkness. The extinction of time . . . By the way, how long has it been? It's stuffy in here. Stifling. What if I never get out and am stuck here forever?

*While* **She** *is fidgeting, she drops her lighter, and the light goes out.*

**She**    Where is the lighter? It was just here, and now it's gone. I shouldn't make a sound, I might get caught . . . . . . What's that smell? Gas. It must be leaking from the lighter. What if it explodes? There isn't enough oxygen here. What do I do? I am claustrophobic . . . I can't breathe. I'm suffocating. Please God, forgive my sins and spare my life. And I will be good. I can't breathe. Mom, please let me out. Help!

*Knocking on the door.* **He** *shouts.*

**He** (*offstage*)    He's gone. You can come out.

**She** (*shouts*)    I'm out of here. I want out. Open the door. Hurry!

**He** (*offstage*)    You should open it. It's locked from within.

**She**    I can't find the lock. It's too dark. Let me out. I'm dying. Open it!

*As* **She** *screams and pounds on the door, there is a sound of a key rattling, being dropped, and rattling again.*

**He** (*offstage*)    Just a minute. Damn. Don't shout, please. You're going to wake up the whole neighborhood.

*The door opens. The stage brightens.* **She**, *covered in tears of fear and completely drained, crawls out to the living room and breathes in the air.*

**He** (*approaching her, worried*)    Are you alright?

**She** (*pushing him away*)    You should have turned on the light. I almost died in there.

**He**    I'm sorry. I forgot. He wasn't a reporter. He said there was a leak in my bathroom, and I managed to stop him from going in there. He said he needed to fix something and . . . Are you okay?

**She**    I was scared to death.

**She** *pushes him away.*

No. I can't do this anymore. It's terrible. I hate this. Why? What is the problem? God, what made me deserve this? Why, of all people, do I have to go through all this? No. I hate to be trapped in this dark tunnel.

**He** (*rubbing her back*)    I'm sorry. It's okay now. I forgot the light in that chaos. It won't happen again. I'll make it all better.

**She**    Make what better? You really messed me up, and now what?

**He**    . . . . . .

**She**    Love? Truth?

**She** *laughs hysterically.*

**He**    Whatever it takes, I'll do it.

**She**    Leave . . . If you can't afford it, I'll help. Don't come back until the rumor goes away. Just be gone forever. Get out! You made my life a mess!

**She** *cries loudly.*

*Blackout.*


**Scene Six**

Setting: Cheongju[16] Bar.

**Friend** *and* **He** *are having* cheongju.

**Friend**    Maybe *cheongju* and this early autumn weather are not such a good match?

**He**    I haven't had much *cheongju*, so I can't say.

**Friend**    This hot *cheongju* is perfect from late autumn on. Just when your breath starts condensing outdoors.

**He**    The first time I had this was when gingko leaves were falling. It was my gap year trying again for college admission, and my father bought me a drink for the first time. He took me to an *Izakaya*,[17] so I thought he'd buy me something fancy. But all he ordered was *cheongju* and gingko nut skewers as a side dish. He said gingko nuts were the perfect match for *cheongju*. Two skewers were all I got.

**Friend**    That's unbelievable. Didn't your appetite hit the roof during the gap year?

**He**    Young people aren't too fond of gingko nuts. They're tough and bitter. Why would anyone eat these? But he would gulp down a glass and eat one nut, and have another glass and then another nut . . . After his third glass he said, "Hang in there, Son. Second time can be the charm."

**Friend**    You must have enjoyed drinking with your father. Usually, fathers and sons don't get along. My husband can't spend ten minutes with his father. They immediately get into an argument. Holidays are a nightmare. My husband moves from room to room just to get away.

**He**    I didn't get to experience that. A few days later, he died from a car accident.

**Friend**    Oh, no.

**He**  . . . . . .

**Friend**  During your gap year?

**He**  Terrible timing. I took another year off. I had to.

**Friend**  And your mother?

**He**  Remarried.

*Slowly taking out his camera.*

I'll take some pictures.

**He** *takes pictures of the gingko nut skewer and the* cheongju *glass.*

**Friend** *looks at him absentmindedly.*

**Friend**  What's your destination?

**He**  I don't know.

**Friend**  But you already booked your flight.

**He**  I just got the cheapest ticket, which was for China. I'll see where I'll be headed from there. Southeast Asia, India, or Russia. It doesn't matter.

**Friend**  It must be dangerous for you to travel alone. Do you have enough money?

**He**  Once I get my lease deposit back, I'll be fine. It's not moving season, so it's taking some time. The landlord says he can't return the deposit until the place is rented out. But it'll be okay.

**She**  Aren't you departing next week? What if your officetel is not rented by then?

**He**  I asked a friend of mine for help.

**She**  So you don't plan ahead.

**He**  . . . Is she doing alright?

**Friend**  People will soon find something else to pay attention to online. Her husband's family made a huge fuss about it for a while. But who cares about them anyway?

**He**  What about her job?

**Friend**  Things need to settle down first. Her show's been pushed to the spring.

**He**  I read about that. She said she only dated me for her story.

**Friend**  Jeez. That must have hurt.

**He**  Is it true?

**Friend**  I don't know. No, I don't think it is. Since the situation's getting out of control, she's handling what's most urgent first. Survival is the priority.

**He**  Why?

**Friend**   . . . . . .?

**He**   Is survival a priority?

**Friend**   Is it not?

**He**   She once said this to me. Women of her generation wanted to live like men. Work, smoke, and drink. Surviving strong. Surviving as the center of the world no matter what it takes. Is that what it is?

**Friend**   That's sarcasm, right?

**He**   I'm not sure. To be frank, I don't even know what went wrong. Was it something I did? Should I be sorry for loving her?

**Friend**   You loved her?

**He**   . . . It seems that way. I know she's strong, self-centered, and even selfish. Maybe I loved her because she's my total opposite. My generation doesn't . . . I mean I don't mind living on the periphery. But for her, that's clearly not enough.

**Friend**   I'm sorry.

**He**   Why are *you*?

*He laughs.*

*Silence.*

**He**   When my father passed away, I had this thought. Life is like a bubble. Nothing comes with certainty. Love feels that way, too . . . But there must be a reason this happened to me. What could have been the truth of our love?

**Friend**   . . . . . .

**He**   I must be drunk. I better get going.

**Friend**   Wait.

*She takes out an envelope from her bag.*

This is from her. To help with your trip.

**He** (*laughs*)   Is it for my service?

**Friend**   Hey, watch your mouth . . .

*She forces the envelope into his pocket.*

You don't need to be embarrassed. She can afford it, and you're still young. She knows she should give it to you herself, but she can't see you right now. Everyone will recognize her, so it's better for her to lie low, right? . . . . . . This might be the best possible ending. Take it as a harsh life lesson and then forget about it. You're a man, after all.

**He**   When the photos and the scandal were all over the internet, she once came to my officetel as white as a ghost. She didn't look like herself. She was trembling with fear and was cold and bitter. And I wondered if I really loved her. Were we ever really in love? . . . I never noticed how much white hair she had. She looked like a strange old lady.

**Friend**    That's what I've been saying. What are you going to do about your age gap? Think about the judgment and finger pointing. Right? It may hurt now, but this is for the best.

**He**    *takes out the envelope and puts it on the table.*

**Friend**    Just take it. You don't even get severance pay as a freelancer.

**He**    . . . . . .

**Friend**    Look. What if you can't find a new tenant?

**He** *gets up.*

**Friend**    Take it. Are you going to starve in China?

**He**    If I take this money, I'm afraid I'll never find out the truth of our love.

**He** *exits.*

**Friend** (*to herself*)    What am I doing here caught in the middle? (*To the waiter.*) Excuse me, can I get another glass of . . . Just bring the whole pot.

*Silence.*

**Friend** *suddenly takes out her phone and calls* **She**.

**Friend**    It's me. I was just with him. He didn't take the money . . . Hey, he has self-respect. If you offer him money and send him abroad like this, he'll surely feel like you're paying him for his service . . . Hey, you. Sometimes you act like a real bitch. You're not the only one who's hurt. How do you think he's feeling right now? He's pathetic. We're all getting dirty in the puddle all the same. We all make mistakes . . . Hey, you got some dirt on you, so what? You've come this far. Everybody makes a mistake and hits rock bottom once in a while. There's no exception. It's not a baseless rumor. It will pass. People don't care about other people's business . . . I know how you feel. You're going crazy. But . . . No, it wasn't him. (*Sighs.*) Listen carefully . . . . . . It was me . . . I spread the rumor . . . Yes, I did it. I'm to blame . . . No, I'm not drunk. Well, a little drunk. That's why I'm telling the truth. Truth. What does that term mean to you? Your young boyfriend is very fond of truth . . . . . . I know I swore I'd never divulge it. But my mouth has a mind of its own. It wasn't my intention to spread it. I was drunk, and it happened . . . Mi-Kyung from the magazine kept talking about him. She said she met him through you. So I thought she knew. You two are close. Once the drink got the best of me, I couldn't stop myself. She kept pushing me for details. Gossips and tabloids, I never thought they would spread so fast . . . Hey, are you there? This got out of control, and it's all because of me . . . I was too afraid to tell you.

*Blackout.*

**Scene Seven**

Setting: Her Officetel.

*She has moved into the officetel that used to be* **His**.

*A little Christmas tree with a mini-bulb tells the season.*

*A television is on. The television announcer summarizes the year in retrospect and reports the upcoming ringing of the bell[18] for the New Year.*

*There are interviews about the upcoming presidential election and the administration of the government.*

*The doorbell rings.*

*Once it lights up,* **She**, *in casual clothing, is facing* **Friend** *in a coat.*

**Friend**    Have you been waiting long? There was a huge crowd waiting for the bell striking around Jongno, and I should have taken the subway.

*Looks at the television.*

Wow, what a mess.

**She** *turns off the television.*

**Friend**    So Myung-Bak Lee is our new President.[19]

**She**    I guess people want stability. Can I take your coat?

**Friend**    I'll only stay a minute.

**She**    How will our descendants evaluate this era? The era that put desire first, over our desperate yearning for democracy? Do you want a glass of wine?

**Friend**    Sure. Is this his officetel?

**She**    Yes. This was the only way to give him some travel money. I also needed a place after I moved out.

**Friend**    Does he call?

**She** (*shakes her head*)    I told him I'd keep my home phone number, but there were no calls. I thought he'd at least call on Christmas. Do you think he's been kidnapped by Manchurian bandits?

**She** *pours the wine.*

*Silence.*

**Friend**    I heard about the divorce. I called your cell, but the number wasn't working.

**She**    I was getting too many annoying calls.

**Friend**    . . . . . .

**She**    The manuscript.

**She** *takes the complete manuscript from the table and hands it to* **Friend**.

**Friend**    You finished it. Despite all the stuff you were going through.

**She**    After I went almost broke from paying for my divorce, I could focus on writing. Is our show still on the table?

**Friend**    Sure. You changed the title. It used to be *The Wind's Desire*.

**She**    The content changed, too. Now it's about the Sampoong Department Store collapse.

**Friend**    What? Why?

**She**    As I kept writing, my mind oftentimes went into total darkness. The darkest place I could imagine was underground.

**Friend**    Wasn't it a romance?

**She**    There are lots of love stories. This is me being unconventional. With a building collapse, covert crony capitalism, and scandals, it will be more suspenseful.

**Friend**    We already did the casting.

**She**    The circumstances are similar in one scene. A young man is stuck under the collapsed department store, and the older heroine is right outside. Would she let her lover die and live her life as if nothing happened? Or would she confess everything to her husband and have her lover rescued?

**Friend**    What does she do?

**She**    What would *you* do?

*Silence.*

**Friend**    You're really upset with me, right?

**She**    It's all water under the bridge. You don't have to stay. Your husband's waiting.

**Friend**    . . . I'm sorry. I didn't mean to do it.

**She**    . . . . . . I hated you for a long time.

**Friend**    . . . . . .

**She**    We've been friends forever, but our friendship took a turn. I couldn't stand your abrupt jumping to conclusions, your excessive compassion, and your fake-candid, but actually condescending, tone anymore. I was sure you spread the rumor on purpose. Subconsciously, yet intentionally.

**Friend**    . . . . . .

**She**    I was in a slump for a long time. My life felt like an unnecessary burden. All the factors that led to this seemed external to me. My husband, my parents, and the world that cannot tell a work of art from hypocrisy. I blamed him at first, and then I blamed you.

**Friend**   Maybe you're right. I deserve the blame this time. Like you said, the revelation was probably intentional, even though I wanted to believe it was a mistake. You know how difficult it is not to spill the beans.

*Silence.*

**Friend** (*sips the wine*)   Let me be frank with you. In addition to divulging your secret, I may have wanted to gossip about you. "How long will this clueless friend keep up this charade? We're all getting old, and she's getting it on with a baby, like she's Juliet."

**She**   Aren't you a little too frank?

**Friend**   It's New Year's Eve. The perfect time for confession.

**She**   . . . . . .

**Friend**   You said earlier that you first hated me and found me uncomfortable. So did I. I found you frustrating and tedious. All self-righteous and inane. Your presence made me feel like a snob. And now this never-do-anything-wrong-prude is having an affair? You, the prime example of plainness, acting like you've got something special going on, like you're pretty. You were that way in high school, too. Do you know how jealous and annoyed I was? But what's that now? You're almost fifty, and you're still all that? Like spring returned only for you?

*The two of them burst out laughing.*

**She**   I lost everything, all thanks to you, bitch.

**Friend** (*laughs*)   I'm sorry. I know I shouldn't laugh, but it's just too funny. It's like we're teenagers.

**She**   . . . . . . It's the New Year soon. Shall we toast?

**Friend**   Sure. Soon it will be a new year.

*They toast.*

**Friend**   Happy New Year!

**She**   Happy New Year!

*Silence.*

**She**   The day I paid for my divorce and went broke, I asked myself what the hell went wrong with me. I blamed God for losing everything just for a little bit of fun. Then all of a sudden, I thought of him. He must be wandering around some strange land with a different language. What would he be thinking about? . . . . . . I must be in love with him. The truth I found, once I had no more desire left and found myself in utter despair, was my love for him. But instead of letting him know, I swore at him and pushed him away, abroad.

**Friend**   I'm sorry.

**She**   I don't deserve that. You threw away friendship, but I threw love right in the garbage can . . . For a long time, I've been afraid to confront myself. I've been keeping a lie deep inside me. I didn't have the courage to admit that my marriage was a failure. As soon as my husband went bankrupt, I didn't even give him a second chance, and sent him away to the U.S. with the excuse of pursuing our daughter's education. I complained that the world wasn't appreciating my writing. But the problem was my talent.

**Friend**    Hey, that's not true. You're being hard on yourself.

**She**    Never mind. Just listen. For once I wanted to face the truth. Even with a friend like you, I couldn't share the truth. Because we also had to work together. I needed to impress you. That's why I hated you more. We've shared great moments caring about each other and supporting each other. But I was so focused on hiding my hatred from you. And I didn't realize how grateful I was to have you in my life.

**Friend**    . . . . . . I'm sorry.

**She**    That's okay. You should go. Your husband must be waiting.

**Friend**    That jerk isn't waiting for me. He'll be back at dawn, completely wasted.

**Friend** *puts on her coat.*

*She picks up the manuscript.*

**Friend**    With Sampoong Department Store, the production cost will be enormous.

**She**    You're the Director of Programming.

**Friend**    We'll create it digitally. Sampoong Department Store, now with a new President, in the era of growth-first. It's not going to be easy.

**She**    I hope you can build a real set.

**Friend**    . . . I owe you big time, so I can't really say no. Cheeky. It's good to see you undaunted. Happy New Year.

**Friend** *leaves, and* **She** *is left alone.*

*Long silence.*

**She**    Undaunted? Yeah, even broke, I am undaunted. Even alone on December 31st, I am undaunted . . . Five minutes to the New Year.

**She** *turns on the television.*

*News about the new President.*

**She** *clicks her tongue, turns off the television, and sits at her computer.*

**She**    New Year's resolution . . . . . . Write. About what? (*Opens her computer.*) . . . The upcoming decadence of desire. Greed and stupidity. Betrayal, a split in friendship, and praying in the dark for the moment of light. The truth of love.

**She** *types on her computer.*

*The telephone rings.*

**She** *stops typing and looks at her phone.*

*The phone lights up.*

*Blackout.*

*End of Play.*


## Notes

1    "Wild goose daddy" (*Gireogi appa*) refers to a father who works in Korea while sending his wife and children to an English-speaking country for the children's education. This play reverses the gender roles.
2    This whole paragraph is a reference to the essay "What Makes Us Sad" ("Was traurig macht") by German poet Anton Schnack, published in *Die Angel des Robinson* (1946).
3    Yeouido [*pronounced Yuh-Uih-Doh*] is a large island on the Han River in Seoul. South Korea, and is Seoul's main finance and investment banking district. It contains the National Assembly Building, the Korea Financial investment Association, the 63 Building, Korean Broadcasting System, and the Korea Exchange Center.
4    Wild goose daddy phenomenon: referring to a father who works in Korea while sending his wife and children to an English-speaking country for the children's education. This play reverses this phenomenon by making the mother a wild goose mom.
5    Reference to Virginia Woolf's quote in her essay on the work and legacy of Montaigne, published in her collection *The Common Reader*: Virginia Woolf, *The Common Reader* (1925). New Delhi: General Press, 2021. pp. 45–46. Full quote: "Here the soul, getting restive, is lashing out at the more palpable forms of Montaigne's great bugbears, convention and ceremony. But watch her as she broods over the fire in the inner room of that tower which, though detached from the main building, has so wide a view over the estate. Really she is the strangest creature in the world, far from heroic, variable as a weathercock, 'bashful, insolent; chaste, lustful; prating, silent; laborious, delicate; ingenious, heavy; melancholic, pleasant; lying, true; knowing, ignorant; liberal, covetous, and prodigal' in short, so complex, so indefinite, corresponding so little to the version which does duty for her in public, that a man might spend his life merely in trying to run her to earth."
6    There is a park by the National Assembly Building, which houses Korea's legislative branch of government. Yeouido is also known for its Cherry Blossom Festival, which usually takes place in early April. Yeouido Park is a popular recreational area, especially for bicycle riding, near the National Assembly Building. But the park She and Friend are at is a less frequented park right next to the building.
7    Yoon-Joong-Ro: The road which winds around the National Assembly Building. It is the main walking course for the Cherry Blossom Festival.
8    *Jjuggumi* (webfoot octopus): A Korean spring delicacy, usually stir-fried with vegetables and marinated in spicy sauce.
9    Soju: A clear and distilled Korean alcohol, with alcohol content about 17%. Because of its refreshing taste and reasonable price, it is the most popular alcoholic beverage alongside Korean food.
10    Hongdae is a region near Hongik University in Seoul and is known for its active night life, with bars, karaoke lounges, and dance clubs.

11  *Patbingsu* [Paht-Bing-Soo] is a traditional Korean summer dessert, literally meaning red bean shaved ice. It is served in a bowl of shaved ice, with toppings including chopped fruit, condensed milk, rice cakes, and matcha powder.

12  Military service is mandatory for able-bodied men in South Korea.

13  Reference to Shakespeare's *Romeo and Juliet*.

14  Reference to an advertisement.

15  The Sampoong Department Store collapsed due to a structural failure on June 29, 1995, in Seoul, South Korea, killing 502 people and injuring 937.

16  *Cheongju*, pronounced Cheong-Joo, is a clear, refined rice wine of Korean origin, which is served hot.

17  Fancy Japanese-style bar.

18  The ringing of the bell at midnight on December 31st is a tradition in Korea, bidding farewell to the previous year and welcoming the New Year with hope. The bell is located in Boshingak bell pavilion in Jongno, which is in downtown Seoul. The bell is rung thirty-three times to commemorate the Joseon Dynasty (1392–1910) tradition of ringing the bell thirty-three times at 4 a.m. to signal the end of the night curfew and start of the new day. Large crowds gather in Jongno to hear the bell ring each New Year's Eve.

19  Myung-Bak Lee served as President from 2008 to 2013. A former CEO of Hyundai Engineering and Construction, Lee focused his presidential campaign on the revitalization of the economy, which was undergoing a serious recession in the late 2000s.

# Bibliography

Beckett, Samuel, *Waiting for Godot: A Tragicomedy in Two Acts*. New York: Grove Press, 2011

Brecht, Bertolt, 1949. "A Short Organum for the Theatre" (1949) in *Brecht on Theatre: The Development of an Aesthetic*. Ed. and trans. John Willett. London: Methuen, 1964

Büchner, Georg, *Dantons Tod* (1835). Leipzig: Reclam Philipp Jun, 1993

Kim, Busik, *Samguk Sagi* (History of the Three Kingdoms, 1145). Ed. and trans. Kang-Lae, Lee. Paju-si: Hangilsa, 1988

Schnack, Anton, "Was traurig macht" in *Die Angel des Robinson*. Desch München, 1946

Shakespeare, William, *Macbeth*. Ed. Kenneth Muir. London: Methuen, 1971

Sophocles, *Oedipus the King*. *Greek Tragedies I, 4th Edition*. Ed. and trans. (from Greek and English into Korean) Woohyun, Cho. Seoul: Hyeonamsa, 1996

Woolf, Virginia, *The Common Reader* (1925). New Delhi: General Press, 2021